God, Are You
Nice or Mean?

I will not leave you as orphans;
I will come to you.

John 14:18

God, Are You Nice or Mean?

Trusting God ... After the Orphanage

Debra Delulio Jones, M Ed

WestBow
PRESS
A DIVISION OF THOMAS NELSON

All Scripture quotations, unless otherwise indicated, are taken from the
Holy Bible, New American Standard Bible. NASB. Copyright © 1960,
1962, 1963, 1968, 1971, 1972, 1973, 1975, 1977 by The Lockman
Foundation, a corporation not for profit, La Habra, California. All
rights reserved. Used by permission of The Lockman Foundation.

WestBow Press books may be ordered through booksellers or by contacting:

WestBow Press
A Division of Thomas Nelson
1663 Liberty Drive
Bloomington, IN 47403
www.westbowpress.com
1-(866) 928-1240

Because of the dynamic nature of the Internet, any web addresses or
links contained in this book may have changed since publication and
may no longer be valid. The views expressed in this work are solely those
of the author and do not necessarily reflect the views of the publisher,
and the publisher hereby disclaims any responsibility for them.

Any people depicted in stock imagery provided by Thinkstock are models,
and such images are being used for illustrative purposes only.

Certain stock imagery © Thinkstock.

ISBN: 978-1-4497-4825-8 (sc)
ISBN: 978-1-4497-4824-1 (e)
Library of Congress Control Number: 2012906789

Printed in the United States of America
WestBow Press rev. date: 5/16/2012

To adoptive moms and dads,
May your journeys with your
"forever families" be blessed
beyond measure.

Acknowledgments

Thank you to my husband, Alan, whose love and dedication are unending. I appreciate the many hours that you flew solo while I labored over the laptop. Many thanks as well for your faithful prayers for me.

A huge thank you also goes to Megan and Dane for your willingness to share the painful moments of your personal journeys so that other families may be helped. You are both so courageous, and I am so glad you are mine.

Thanks to Mom and Dad and my brother, Ronny, because you are proud of me no matter what I set out to do.

Special thanks to my friends at The TCU Institute of Child Development. I shudder to think what this journey may have been like were it not for you and your dedication to serving adoptive and foster families. I am forever grateful that you were the lives God used to be our rescue team. Thank you for your continued hard work and commitment to kids from "hard places."

Finally, to my friends who prayed, brainstormed, and read manuscripts to keep me on track, I thank you. I am so blessed to have you in my life.

Introduction

"Truly I tell you, unless you are converted
and become like children,
you shall not enter the kingdom of heaven." Matthew 18:3

God, are you nice or mean? Sounds like something a small child would say, doesn't it? Well, that's exactly how I felt ten years ago—like a small child—scared, inadequate, without hope, and wanting a parent to hold me in his arms. My earthly parents had comforted me plenty of times during our difficult parenting journey with our troubled son whom we adopted from Romania, but what I needed was divine intervention. I needed to know if the God I'd put my faith in was going to come through in my darkest hour. Like a child, I screamed at him asking if he was nice or mean, but I was really asking, "God, can I trust you?"

In case you want to send me an email chastising me for being irreverent with this book title, please understand that I am well aware of the God-fearing verses. I know he is the God of the universe, and he could squish me like a bug if he chose to. He is holy, all-powerful, all-knowing, and is sovereign. My heart was not intentionally disrespectful or dishonoring toward God in any way, but desperate for understanding. The only way I could come to him was in complete honesty and baring my soul like a wounded child. He already knew what I was feeling, and I figured he was big enough to handle my being furious with him.

I was surrounded by loving friends at church, many with words of encouragement and hope. I was grateful for them and wouldn't have made it without them, but at my lowest low, I didn't need trite answers from church-goers, I needed my heavenly daddy. I needed to hear from him. I cried out to him in childlike faith, begging him to answer, and he did.

Perhaps you are a parent on a difficult journey, and you grabbed this book because you have adopted a child with a background of abandonment, neglect, abuse, or trauma. Maybe your painful adoption journey has caused you to question whether you misunderstood what you once believed was a call of God on your life to complete your family through the gift of adoption. Your hard times have possibly caused you to question the goodness of a God who would allow thousands of babies to be abandoned in deplorable conditions or who allows small children to become victims of horrendous sexual and physical abuse.

I don't pretend to have all the answers to the questions men and women have struggled with for centuries regarding human suffering and a loving God. I do know this, my God is faithful. My God hears when we cry out to him. And my God will work all things for good to those who love him and are called according to his purpose (Romans 8:28).

Whether you are a struggling parent or feel like a spiritual orphan because of your own painful life experiences that you cannot make sense of, I invite you to take a journey with me to a story of restoration. It is my story, but it is also my husband Alan's story; my daughter Megan's story; and my son Dane's story. I ask that you handle it with care, for these are the dearest people in my life.

Chapter 1

. . . .

Another Baby

The doctor's words haunted me. "And by the way, don't plan on having any more children." I burst into tears as he nonchalantly turned to leave my hospital room.

At that time I was a twenty-seven-year-old, high-energy mother who had recently resigned my special education position to be a full-time mommy. My baby girl, Megan, had just turned one year old, and I was thrilled to be home with her. I was working part-time in direct sales and had some ambitious personal goals in mind.

Needless to say, those goals didn't include double vision and complete paralysis on the right side of my body. I was so shocked that I was in the hospital at all, and even more shocked to learn I had multiple sclerosis. My husband, Alan, tried to be strong for both of us, but I knew he was devastated as well. Seeing his strong-willed, fun-loving, determined wife in such a weakened state was foreign to him. The final blow of being told that I wouldn't be able to have more children was heartbreaking.

I loved being a mom, and my plans definitely included having another baby in a couple of years. It seemed unreal that I had a lifelong battle ahead of me with a mysterious, unpredictable disease for which there was no cure. That news coupled with doctor's orders not to risk a second pregnancy which might exacerbate another MS attack was more than I could bear.

My diagnosis was the relapsing/remitting form of the disease which meant it might go into remission or it might not. I might go years without another attack or I might have another one tomorrow. My vision might return to normal or I might go blind. I might be left with mild damage or I might never get out of this wheelchair. The symptoms could affect any area of my body, including cognitive impairment. The list of unknowns seemed longer than what was known of this illness.

My faith in God was my only hope. I was in the habit of reading a Proverb a day correlating with the days of the month. It was November 3 so I turned to Proverbs 3. I clung to the words of verses 5 and 6.

> Trust in the Lord with all your heart
> and do not lean on your own understanding.
> In all your ways acknowledge Him
> and He will make your paths straight.

As I leaned on God, my faith grew to hope, and my hope turned to praise. I'd certainly never pictured myself in a wheelchair with a one-year-old baby during my mid-twenties, but I committed my future to the God I loved. "God, I know you love me, and you know I love you. I'll serve you walking or I'll serve you riding. Let your will be done. I'm yours."

Within days my strength was returning, and I was bouncing around the rehab unit of the hospital. Bouncing as much as you can with a cane that is! Most of my rehab-mates were elderly patients such as stroke victims, with a couple of exceptions like my new friend who'd suffered paralysis due to a spinal cord injury. They watched in amazement as I recovered right before their eyes, and I was praising the Lord to anyone who'd listen. The doctor warned that euphoria could be a symptom of MS. I think I told him to "Just hush," and that I was simply excited at how God was answering my prayers.

I soon walked out of that hospital with the help of my new wooden companion. It wasn't long before I was enjoying life full speed ahead, caneless, busy taking care of Megan and working part-time. I didn't know if I was healed or in remission as the neurologist had stated, but I was praising God either way.

Life returned to normal and in a couple of years I was still symptom free. I began to get the mommy itch and wanted to return to my plan to have a second child. I felt great. I thought and thought. *Maybe they made a mistake. Perhaps I never even had MS or maybe God just healed me. Please, Lord, I want to have another baby. I'm strong now.* I could almost hear Helen Reddy singing "I am woman, hear me roar" in the background of my mind.

About that time, our dear friends had felt the call of God to adopt an orphan from Romania. The plight of the

Romanian orphans was all over the news in the months following the revolution and fall of the dictator, Nicolae Ceausescu. Thousands of innocent victims in deplorable conditions had no one to love and care for them. Most orphanages had ratios of thirty babies to one worker. The more I learned, the more I wondered if adoption could be for us.

I would have never even considered adoption before and had no idea how Alan would react. As I prayed about the possibility, it seemed to make sense. Adoption would save the stress on my body just in case I was experiencing a remission rather than a healing. I wanted to believe I was healed, but those words from my hospital room echoed in my head. What if I had another baby and it caused a relapse? How would I manage a newborn and a preschooler if I ended up in a wheelchair or an even worse condition?

I got up the nerve to talk to Alan about my feeling that God was possibly leading us to adopt one of those orphaned babies in Romania. To my surprise he was receptive to the idea, and we both began to pray diligently about it.

We truly believed adoption was God's will for completing our family. There were thousands of children who needed loving Christian homes. I wouldn't be disobeying doctor's orders or putting unnecessary physical stress on myself and risking an MS relapse. It seemed like a perfect answer to our prayers, and we were completely at peace with our decision.

We now call this answer to our prayers our "God comedy." As the saying goes, if you want to make God laugh, tell him your plans. We believed God directed us to international adoption to complete our family and prevent any relapse of MS. Twenty years ago there was little information available on the effects of early trauma or neglect, Eastern European adoptions were in their infancy stage, and there was no Internet. I knew as a special educator there would be developmental delays, but I felt confident that I knew what to do about that with my master's degree in Language and Learning Disabilities. We thought we were preventing stress which is the biggest enemy of an MS patient. We had no clue of the intense stress and trauma we were about to bring into our family.

Chapter 2

· · · · · · · · · ·

Headed to Romania

"I can't believe I'm on this plane," I managed to say to Alan as I tried to catch my breath. Our flight plans had been abruptly changed due to the outbreak of war in Yugoslavia. "Guess we're not flying into Yugoslavia and then connecting to Romania, huh?" I asked Alan. I wondered whether or not to share with my parents that we were headed near a war zone in Eastern Europe.

Our next option was to fly from Dallas to New York, then catch Tarom, the Romanian airline. What we didn't know was that Tarom was run quite differently from the airlines we were accustomed to in the States. It was not exactly the level of customer service we were used to. Not only did they not mail us the tickets we were promised, there was no one to answer the phone when I called to inquire about our connecting flight from New York to Romania. And I mean they wouldn't answer their phone, ever, for days—many days.

We had our tickets to New York confirmed with a major US airline, but had no idea if we would have tickets for our flight to Romania once we got to LaGuardia. I decided the only way to find out was to fly to New York and ask in person at the Tarom ticket counter. If we didn't have tickets, we'd buy them there and catch the next flight available. I made arrangements for my New Yorker cousin, Dale, to pick us up and we'd stay with him and my aunt until we could catch the next flight out on Tarom.

When we arrived, Alan and Dale piled our massive luggage into what felt like a "Little Tikes" car and drove to another terminal to locate Tarom Airlines. We would not have time to catch the original flight even if we did somehow have tickets, or so we thought.

As we approached the ticket counter, it looked like total chaos with people swarming everywhere, most of them not speaking my language. My teeth nearly fell out when before we even reached the desk, I heard a voice in a thick Romanian accent yelling, "Debra Jones! Debra and Alan Jones?"

What? Someone here knows we exist? As we made our way through the crowd, the lady calling our names was frantically waving two tickets in the air and shouting, "Go, go! Your flight will leave!"

Unbelievable! I turned to my cousin and said, "Hurry! Get those bags out of the car. We're going to get our baby!"

Running with all our might, we blew a kiss to Dale and made it to the gate just in time. We collapsed into our seats huffing and puffing, the last to enter the plane. I couldn't believe we actually pulled it off and were setting out on our venture. God knew all along, and I have to wonder if he was smiling and thinking, "You think *that* was chaotic? I have so much to teach you, my child."

I was so excited and nervous and concerned and sleep deprived and curious, and, and, and . . . .

My thoughts raced about what this journey might entail. I wondered who our baby would be and what God's plan was for our family. I thought I'd never be able to have a second child, but God had provided a way. I knew I should try to sleep because of the fourteen-hour flight and the eight-hour time difference, but my thoughts refused to quiet down and wouldn't obey even my toughest teacher voice inside my head.

It takes nine months to bring a baby into this world, but in a little over four months we had:

* Felt the heartache of an orphan crisis;
* Prayed to God for wisdom and direction;
* Made a decision to complete our family through adoption;
* Filled out mounds of paperwork;
* Survived the bureaucracy of the US Immigration and Naturalization Service;
* And caught a plane to a slightly post-communist country.

I say "slightly" post-communist because sixteen months after the revolution, evidence of political unrest was all around us when we got there. As our flight arrived, I was filled with anticipation and anxiety. I tried to picture in my mind what I would experience in one of the poorest countries in Europe. Nowadays I would have just Googled it, but I didn't have that luxury in 1991.

I don't think even Internet scenes would have prepared me for the next few moments. As I placed my feet onto the tarmac, I felt like I was entering the Twilight Zone. My surroundings seemed more like I was in the World War II time period.

The airport was dark and gloomy. Uniformed, armed, military guards lined the premises. We were soon bodily frisked, which was something I'd never experienced since this was a decade prior to 9-11. We approached the international passenger's window where we were ordered to show our passports. After passing that checkpoint, our suitcases were flung open and searched. As the guard rummaged through diapers, bottles, and our clothes, he discovered about forty Bibles we'd brought to offer as gifts to our soon-to-be Romanian friends. "What's this?" he demanded. *I sure would miss freedom,* I thought, wondering if I was about to be locked up. "Bibles. It's okay?" I questioned, as my heart was beating up the inside of my chest. "Okay," he blurted and pointed us on our way.

Whew! I had no idea that my first twenty minutes in this country would be so stressful. I made a mental note of what *not* to tell my mother.

We later learned that the president of France was scheduled to arrive that day, thus the extra military presence. I was relieved to know all those guards weren't there just for the Joneses!

Outside the airport, we found the people of Romania to be warm, friendly, and welcoming of Americans. We would spend many hours in the days to come conversing over long dinners and felt very safe in the homes of our new friends. They wanted to know everything about our lives in America, and they loved to talk about President Reagan and his stand against communism. We'd occasionally see political riots in the streets and once again a heavy military presence. Our friends would put their arms around us like parents and steer us through the uproar.

Our days were filled with praying and searching for the baby who would become our new son or daughter. How would we know? What would we feel?

What we didn't know until we got to Bucharest was that the Romanian government was soon to put a stop to all adoptions due to a great deal of corruption in the process. In fact, there were many orphanages that wouldn't allow foreigners to visit at all due to the uncertainty and rumors that private adoptions would be halted. This greatly complicated the search for our new baby.

We found out you had to know someone who had specific knowledge of an orphan whose birth parents could be located. They were then contacted to determine if they'd be willing to relinquish their parental rights since they'd already abandoned their child. If they agreed, a petition was filed and a court date set for a private adoption. This would be unheard of today.

In our searching, we became discouraged and began to fear we'd be coming home without a baby. After several exhausting days, late one night I looked at Alan and asked, "What are we doing here?" I was in such culture shock, was so homesick, and my heart ached for Megan. The scars of communism left a spiritual darkness in this land that was so heavy I could feel it. I just wanted to do what

I believed was God's will and give a permanent, loving home to an orphaned child, but it was beginning to look like we were too late. The government was cracking down on private adoptions, although there were no agencies in place at that time that provided a better way to adopt these children.

Finally, through a series of what seemed like divine appointments, we were led to meet Ionel Ungureauneau, a tiny little guy with a huge toothless grin. He was ten months old, but weighed only about twelve pounds and was developmentally more like a three-month-old. He was so weak from malnourishment and had a severe diaper rash from lying in soaking wet, cloth diapers. That was the harsh reality of thirty babies to one caregiver. His tiny, frail body had more rashes on the sides of his neck as formula ran down his cheeks from the propped bottles. He didn't have the strength to suck from the bottles I brought from home. *How does a baby unlearn the instinct of sucking?* I went back to the orphanage to see what I could find out and they gave me one of their bottles which had a huge hole cut in the nipple so the watered-down formula flowed like a water fountain. Little Ionel had survived much in his few short months in this life.

I know it sounds cliché, but I just knew the moment I held him that he was the one. Alan felt the same way. We were absolutely smitten and couldn't wait to bring him home to meet his big sister, Megan, and become part of his forever family.

Of course more paperwork, bureaucracy, and a court date came first. Alan had to get back to his teaching job and to Megan who had been staying with my parents, so I kissed him goodbye and put him on the plane. I'd stay another three weeks or so to finalize the adoption and immigration process. Alan recalls that getting on that plane and leaving me alone in Romania was the hardest thing he's ever done. I was determined to do whatever it took to take care of Dane Anthony, whom we'd officially rename shortly.

May 15 was our court appearance. Dane's birth parents appeared before the judge and signed their relinquishment papers with thumbprints. I knew they were poor and uneducated from the harsh system they'd survived, but I didn't realize they wouldn't even know how to sign their names. My heart sank, and I wondered what they must be feeling—surely sad that they'd never see him again. Or were they happy that he wouldn't have to endure what they had lived.

Outside the court, they met with us briefly for a couple of pictures, and through an interpreter I assured them that I would give him the best life possible. Victoria Ungureauneau shed a quiet tear as she hugged Ionel for the last time. He was the sixth child in her impoverished family, and she knew there was no way they could care for him. Their former dictator had forced all women of childbearing age to have at least five children or suffer the consequences of huge taxes they couldn't pay. That's what led to the thousands of orphans here, but seeing it played out in real life hit me like an ice pick piercing my heart. I only thought I understood when I sobbed through the documentaries I'd seen back home. The bittersweet emotions were overwhelming for me.

When I got back to the home of the family who had helped us find Dane, I was in for more heart piercing. My new Romanian friends were all watching the evening news with arms flailing and reacting with such outrage and emotion that I knew something horrible was happening. Of course they were speaking Romanian, and no one was taking the time to translate for me. "What? What? Someone please tell me what is going on."

My friend, Radu, explained that they had just announced that the Romanian government had put a freeze on all adoptions. No more children could be adopted until a government list of those who were available for adoption was compiled. This would take several months. Many families were awaiting court dates, and it was unknown whether or not those who had already filed petitions for adoption would be able to bring their children home. "You are so lucky you got Dane today," Radu announced. I was certain there was no "luck" to it and was so thankful that God had brought me to this place in the journey.

What a day it had been! Back in my tiny little room in a Romanian flat, I sat all alone on a twin bed, thousands of miles away from my family. I looked at my new son's makeshift crib of two living room chairs pushed together. I held him tight as I thought of some of the Americans I'd befriended who might not get to finalize the adoptions of the children they'd already fallen in love with. I was overcome with emotion as I sang to my new baby, "Jesus loves the little children, all the children of the world. Red and yellow, black and white, they . . . are . . . precious . . . in . . . his . . . sight . . . ." I could no longer sing through my weeping. I didn't get it. I couldn't begin to understand. It was too much.

"God, this is so unfair! If they are precious in your sight, why are they here in these horrible conditions? There are thousands of them. I know that you didn't do it, but why would you even allow it? And now that there are people willing to adopt them, why shouldn't they get to be rescued through adoption? My head can't wrap around all of this. Yet, I'm so grateful for my baby son. I love you and thank you." Trying to pull myself together, I looked at my new baby, now safe in my arms and wondered, *And why you? Why out of thousands, do you get to be the one plucked out of here?*

I sensed that still small voice of God telling me in the quiet of my mind to trust him. "I have a special plan for this one."

Chapter 3

. . . .

Welcome Home

Red, white, and blue balloons and patriotic T-shirts made this day a memorable photo moment. A crowd of family and friends gathered at the airport to welcome Dane to America. Alan and I immediately introduced him to his new big sister, and the grandparents couldn't wait to hold the new baby. We felt like now our "happily ever after" could begin. Three weeks after he came home, we celebrated his first birthday.

He seemed to be an easy baby. He slept through the night and rarely cried. While it was nice to not have to worry about 2:00 a.m. feedings, deep down I knew that the reason he didn't cry was because he had experienced many months of no one coming to the sound of his voice. I wanted him to know that I would always be there.

We settled into our new routine, and Megan was proud to show everyone her new baby brother. She did have a few jealous three-year-old moments, and I reminded myself that all this came into her life so fast. I tried to hide my laughter when she in no uncertain terms told us, "I want the new baby to sleep in the garage!"

I was well aware that Dane had some catching up to do so I set out to fatten him up and work on the significant developmental delays. My special education and child development training came in handy, and I sought help from Early Childhood Intervention soon after Dane came home. Early Childhood Intervention is a statewide program for families with children, birth to age three, with disabilities and developmental delays. Their goal and mine was to remediate the gap between his developmental age of three months and his chronological age of twelve months.

Healthy nutrition and an environment where he could thrive seemed to be paying off. I was amazed at how quickly he was gaining weight and growing. We were thrilled when he passed zero on the growth chart at the pediatrician's office. He was still tiny, but at least he was out of the negative numbers.

Daily we worked on activities to strengthen his weak muscles and develop his motor skills. Our homework appeared to be paying off, and by sixteen months of age he was walking and talking. When Dane was eighteen months old, an adoptive mom I'd connected with in Romania brought her eight-month-old baby to visit, and we reminisced about our tense moments and adoption adventures in Romania. Both of us were thrilled that our adoptees were overcoming the rough starts they'd had in life and were thriving in our homes.

By age two, Dane no longer was a baby who didn't cry. In fact, crying and tantrums were becoming quite frequent, but I didn't think too much about it. Terrible twos were normal on the developmental scales, and he definitely had the verbal skills to say, "NO!" He was very hyper, and I was completely worn out by the end of each day. My friends told me boys are just different, and I shouldn't compare him to my sweet little girl when she was that age. I thought, *They're different, all right!*

Terrible twos turned into terrible threes, and I was becoming concerned. My experience as a special education teacher was leading me to believe we had some issues here. He was extremely hyperactive and would often run away from us. Tantrums were prolonged and severe. He had uncontrollable rage. I wondered how such a young child could have so much anger. Sleep was also an issue. Alan and I would spend hours getting him settled down enough to go to sleep, many times well after midnight. The exhaustion and stress of Dane's behavior was taking a toll on the family.

At his three-year-old checkup, I spoke with his pediatrician about these behaviors. She didn't seem overly concerned and even commented that I was a little hyper myself. She recommended slowing our lifestyle down a bit and sticking with a consistent routine. I remember thinking, *Surely these severe behaviors can't be all my fault, but I'll pull back on some of our activities and see if that helps.*

Slowing down didn't make any difference. It was like we had two kids in one body with Dane. At times he seemed loving, affectionate, and wanted to please us. At the other extreme, he would hit, bite, spit, kick, scream, yell, threaten, and throw things at us. I read parenting books by leading experts who were well-respected in the field of Christian parenting, but had no results with any of the suggestions in the books.

Time out seemed to be the most popular method of dealing with three-year-old tantrums according to several experts, but the books didn't tell you what to do if he wouldn't stay there. They surely didn't indicate what to do if he threw the time-out chair at your head!

Alan had little patience with him, and mine was wearing out fast. Megan was in kindergarten by this time, and we were feeling like she was getting less and less of our time and attention because there was usually a Dane crisis going on. These ranged from his destructive behaviors around the house, constantly getting into everything just because he was so hyper to episodes where he would purposely tear something up in a fit of rage. We nicknamed it Dane-a-mania.

Long days of constant fits and late nights seemed to have no end in sight. We would be so tired at the end of the day, only to face the endless battle of getting him to sleep. He was either bouncing off the walls almost in a drunken state or raging because he didn't want to go to bed.

I remember bursting out one day during prayer request time at my ladies' Bible study. "The books don't tell you what to do when he wads up your contact lens and leaves it out to dry! And we can't get any rest." I knew I couldn't take much more and at church I had been labeled the one with the patience of Job.

My part-time career in direct sales was becoming impossible to continue. I couldn't slip into the spare bedroom to make phone calls with him screaming in the background. And babysitters were difficult to keep so I could work a few hours during the day. What was a mom to do?

We tried to press on the best way we knew how, but life was not fun. The constant stress in our home was becoming unmanageable. If we went out, we were sure to have an embarrassing public scene, and I was sick of the stares and glares with people seeming to look at me as if I were a bad parent. Sometimes I'd even hear comments from complete strangers about what they'd do if their child acted like that. *UGH! Lord, let me never judge someone for how their child behaves, because I have no idea what might be going on in their lives.*

By Dane's four-year-old checkup, I begged the pediatrician for help. By that time she was convinced the problem was not my active lifestyle, and referred me to a psychologist. I have to say I felt sorry for the young man. As Dane destroyed his office, I filled out the questionnaires listing all Dane's horrible behaviors and thought this poor psychologist will earn his money today!

He asked to take Dane back to his office alone. I agreed and in my heart was thinking, *You'll be back for me soon. You'll need the help.* Nevertheless, I was just happy to have a few minutes to read a book in peace.

I thought of Megan and how she was lucky to be at school for seven hours a day and get out of this hell. Poor child, I never knew adopting a baby would bring so much stress into our home. I felt guilty, but I loved them both and God had obviously given Dane to us for a purpose.

It was so humorous to me that we thought we were saving the stress on my MS. I was certain I was healed by this point because it had been nearly six years since I was sick. Surely if I had MS, I would have had a relapse by now with all this stress and drama in my life. I found myself bantering with God. "You were pretty slick. You must have known not many people would have survived Dane, so you tricked me into thinking I had MS so I'd help him. Surely not, but I can't for the life of me figure out what your plan is in all this."

Just as I'd predicted, the psychologist was back within minutes asking me to join them in his office. He looked at me with all seriousness and said, "He has a lot of anger." I contained my sarcasm and agreed that he did. Secretly I wanted to shout, *No joke, Einstein! How much am I paying you to figure that out?*

It was obvious that the unsuspecting, young Ph. D. had met his match with Dane, and he quickly referred me to a psychiatrist. I didn't really blame him. By this time I'd concluded that some weighty psychiatric labels would be coming our way. I'd tried to deny it. I'd tried to avoid the emotionally disturbed diagnoses that I knew made teachers cringe. I'd hoped God would answer my prayers and heal my son. And I'd done everything that I knew to do from my special education training. I looked at my degrees hanging on the wall and whispered to them that they were not enough.

The psychiatrist was a woman with more experience than the young guy we'd recently seen. As Dane tore up her waiting room, I filled out more papers. She'd seen it all before and gave him the diagnosis of Attention Deficit Hyperactivity Disorder (ADHD) and Oppositional Defiant Disorder (ODD). This, of course, led to the prescription pad, and she started him on a popular stimulant medication. They weren't indicated for children less than six years of age, but she knew we were desperate. She prescribed it for our four-year-old. I thought he was awfully young for psychotropic drugs, but at this point it was him or me. I thought if he didn't get help I was headed for the someplace where they'd put me in a padded room.

The day after he started his medication went relatively smooth. I thought perhaps I'd been wrong to try to put this off and maybe we could now have some peace. We actually had a couple of decent weeks, and I thought I might even get some work done now. But I was mistaken.

About three weeks after starting his medication, Dane began having episodes of rage that were worse than before, and that was saying something! His rages would last for three hours or longer. His aggression was even more severe. He chased me around the house with scissors one day and at one point even tried to throw himself out of a moving car. How on earth could a four-year-old display this much rage? I went back to the psychiatrist, and she switched him to a different stimulant medication.

Almost the exact same thing happened. He was great for a couple of weeks, and then went bonkers. Back to the doctor, and she tried another one with almost identical results. At this point, she began to wonder if he was having some type of temporal lobe seizure disorder because stimulants could trigger seizure activity, so she referred us to a pediatric neurologist.

This time I wised up and took my loyal friend, Theresa, so the waiting room wouldn't be destroyed. She could manhandle Dane while I again answered pages of questions about his behavior. After a full day of testing and an EEG, this doctor concluded no seizure activity, but possibly alcohol exposure in utero which could result in brain damage and severe behavior disorders. I asked him what we were going to do. I'll never forget his curt answer. He said there wasn't a lot that helped, but ended his comments with, "You don't have a gun, do you? It's not a good idea with these guys around."

I couldn't get out of there fast enough. *You don't have a gun, do you?* I echoed in my head. *Who says stuff like that? Was this guy telling me my child might grow up and shoot me? Are we in danger? He's four, for Pete's sake! Does no one have any answers that can help my son and our family? Lord, where do I go from here?*

When I finally got Dane to bed that night, I cried and cried. I dumped all this on Alan who was equally exasperated. We were both so exhausted, frustrated, and now fearful of our future for Dane and the entire family. How much can a family take and what's next for us?

Back at the psychiatrist's office I unloaded my fears. She added the diagnosis of severe depression and admitted

Dane to a psychiatric day hospital for observation and some trials of other medication options. They operated on a well-known behavior level system which had proven successful with many children. I have to say I didn't get my hopes up, and their behavior system didn't work any better than the ones I'd tried at home. The psychiatrist did try some different medication combinations that made a slight difference, but it always seemed they didn't work for long.

I knew he was still behind in language and fine motor skills as well and school was going to be another nightmare for us. I dreaded the whole thing and was losing hope, but continued to seek answers. I loved Dane so much and wanted to give him a good life. I was trying everything I knew and then some, but it wasn't enough. As his fifth birthday approached I was nauseated by the thought of kindergarten. I knew he wasn't ready. Do I hold him back? Do I put him in Special Ed? With these behaviors he wasn't going to learn much anywhere.

And what about the rest of us? My income was dwindling because I had very little time or energy to work with all this chaos in our lives. Alan looked angry most of the time, and I was frustrated that he didn't help me more with Dane, but knew he didn't know what to do. Megan now had a lock on her bedroom door to keep her little brother from destroying her things, but it wasn't her things I was worried about. What was all this doing to her? I never intended to bring pain and embarrassment into her life. I never intended to have less time to spend with her because of the needs of her brother. How would we cope as a family?

Cope. I didn't want to just cope. I needed hope!

Chapter 4

· · · · · · · · · ·

A Block of Hope

Coping was our way of life. Doctors, medications, therapists, counselors, special educators, and behaviorists were part of daily living. Family life was still barely manageable, and we earned the most "frequent flyer miles" on the weekly prayer list at Sunday school.

One day a friend called to tell me she'd seen a program on TV that talked about severe behavior problems being related to allergies in children. She recommended I read, *Is This Your Child* by Doris Rapp. I got the book and read about many children with outbursts similar to Dane's. The author explained that these behaviors were often caused by allergies. However, since rages and meltdowns were not the typical upper respiratory symptoms, most parents didn't seek testing and treatment for food or environmental sensitivities.

I was willing to try anything. I took the book to Dane's psychiatrist, and she said it might be worth a try since nothing else seemed to make a significant difference for very long with Dane. I found a doctor who did the type of provocation/neutralization testing needed to diagnose these behavioral allergies. Her name was Dr. Mary Ann Block at The Block Center in Hurst, Texas.

The testing day opened my eyes to a whole new look at behaviors. The nurse would inject a single potential allergen just under the skin on Dane's arm. I was given instructions to watch for any changes in behavior or physical symptoms. The nurse noted changes in the skin reaction. Then neutralizing doses would be injected one at a time until she found the strength that would reverse the reaction. I could not believe what I observed.

Dane would be calm and playing well prior to the testing. Then a single allergen, such as milk, would be injected just under the skin. Almost immediately he'd start throwing toys, yelling and calling me "Stupid." As I tried to contain his behaviors, he'd become more aggressive. The nurse would then inject a neutralizing dose of the same allergen, and Dane would begin to calm down immediately, hop up in my lap and say, "I love you, Mommy!"

Some allergens caused aggressive behaviors. Others, such as sugar, caused him to be silly and wild, almost as if he were drunk. I was watching all the extremes of behavior we'd dealt with for several years being turned on and off as if by a switch.

It was remarkable. Was it possible that we'd been trying to use discipline and psychotropic medications to treat behaviors that were being triggered by allergens? Dane's early malnourishment and neglect certainly could have led to the weakened immune system that would have made him susceptible to allergies. Had I finally found a doctor who had answers that would make a lasting difference?

By the end of testing, the list of foods and environmental allergens that were problematic for Dane was long. He was allergic to almost everything he ate on a regular basis as well as many pollens, grasses, fragrances, and dust. I looked back on behavioral episodes which now made sense. He'd be fine one minute, then when we walked by the fragrance counter at a department store, he'd go nuts and we'd have to leave the mall. I now knew he'd had a reaction to the colognes and perfumes. No wonder it seemed like we had two kids in one body. We also learned from Dr. Block that he had low blood sugar, so we made sure he had protein snacks every two to three hours which helped with his severe mood swings.

We now had a glimmer of hope, but avoiding all of those allergens in his diet and environment was not easy with a strong-willed five-year-old. I was increasingly aware of how much our world revolves around food. Every celebration, school event, or church fellowship posed a problem for Dane.

Armed with allergy shots and a four-day rotation diet, I set out to help my child in a new way. It would not be easy, but the way we were living with all the chaos, rage, and aggression wasn't easy either. I color-coded every food in my pantry right down to the cooking oils, so that Dane would not have the same food more than once in a four-day period. I planned detailed menus and spent much time shopping at health food stores for alternative foods that didn't include the common allergens. The real trick was finding the ones that met that criteria, but didn't taste like cardboard. Dane still had meltdowns if things didn't go his way or if he was out of his routine, but he didn't seem to have as many. Life was hard, but we at least felt like we were making some headway.

Dr. Block introduced us to a new treatment for allergies called Enzyme Potentiated Desensitization (EPD). It had been used in Europe and some patients reported being allergy-free for over twenty years as a result. EPD was in a trial phase in the United States for FDA approval. Since Dane had so many allergens that it was impossible to avoid them all, Dr. Block felt he would be a good candidate for EPD.

With EPD, the patient must be in a strict allergy-free environment around the time of the injection or he is at risk for becoming sensitized to even more allergens. The patient would have an allergy shot every eight weeks initially and as symptoms subsided, he could go longer between injections and had the possibility of even being cured.

In preparation for his EPD injection, we had to make sure he wasn't exposed to anything which had even a slight chance of causing a reaction for several days before and after his injection. It was a very involved schedule, but the day before, the day of, and the day after his shot were most critical. Because we had a dog and a cat, we chose to take him to a hotel for those three days. I made arrangements for our room to be cleaned with fragrance-free products which I provided in advance. We ordered special soap and shampoo for the whole family as well so he wouldn't react to any fragrances.

Dane was on a rigid diet during those three days. He had to have food that was never in his diet, such as lamb and tapioca bagels. I cooked ahead of time and packed his limited choices in an ice chest so we could microwave his meals at the hotel. We loaded up with movies and games and headed to our sterile environment.

The only time we left was for the trip to Dr. Block's office on day two of our exile. Alan would relieve me each evening so I could spend time with Megan and grab a bite of dinner. I just didn't have the heart to eat in front of Dane. Enzyme Potentiated Desensitization was quite an ordeal, but we considered it a temporary sacrifice for a long-term goal. It was worth it to us if it would help our son get well and would alleviate these behavioral reactions. We all hoped it would work.

Dane's behavior improved significantly after his first injection, but it wore off within about three weeks as expected. Eight weeks later we were back for his next treatment. I'm quite sure our friends and his teachers thought we were crazy to be going through all of this, but then again, they hadn't lived in Dane-a-mania. We'd finally been given hope, and we were willing to work hard to see it through.

Dane's improvement continued with each injection, and he reached the point of going a whole year between injections. There were still challenges and power struggles, but his behavior was much more manageable. Unfortunately, EPD did not receive FDA approval and by the next year when he needed another injection, it was no longer available in the States. Some patients were going to Canada for their shots, but that wasn't in our school teacher budget.

By this point in our journey, I had resigned my director position in sales and returned to teaching special education. It was impossible to have a home office with Dane's behavioral meltdowns. I felt I needed to work when he was in school, and my teaching career allowed me to be on his schedule. It was difficult and exhausting, however, because I taught Special Ed all day and lived it all night. I wondered how long I'd be able to go on like this and if our family would survive the increasing challenges that came as Dane grew too big to contain in an aggressive rage.

We respect and admire Dr. Mary Ann Block so much and are to this day thankful for all she taught us. Not all children have to go on the strict rotation diet, and for some, neutralizing shots or even drops are all they need. There are also new allergy options now available as well as ongoing research. I often refer parents to Dr. Block when they are seeking answers to their child's troubling behavior. We continued to avoid Dane's allergens as much as possible, but it became apparent at this point in our parenting journey that he had other complex and multiple, overlapping issues that also needed to be addressed. It was time to look for additional answers once more.

Chapter 5

· · · · · · · · · ·

Hope at Hope Connection

Dane's behavior continued to decline and our frustrations continued to increase. We tried psychiatry once more, but were unable to have any success with the medications. I knew Dr. Block would cringe if she knew what medications were being considered. Some that were recommended had side effects so severe that I just wasn't willing to take the risk with my nine-year-old. As he'd gotten older, it was so hard to control his diet. The power struggles over food became more severe than the benefit we received from avoiding them. I was completely worn out trying to manage all of this.

The previous summer, we'd taken Dane to a research-based day camp for troubled adopted kids called Hope Connection at Texas Christian University. Karyn Purvis was the director and at that time was a student working on her PhD in Developmental Psychology under the direction of Dr. David Cross. Karyn had a way with these out-of-control kids like no one I'd ever seen. From her ongoing research, she taught us so much about the behaviors of children from backgrounds of neglect, abandonment, abuse, or other traumas. Her gentle, yet firm way of teaching kids from "hard places" as she called them, was an answer to our prayers. She seemed to peer right into their souls. Quite frankly, I was just as grateful for the respite during the hours he was at camp for those few weeks.

At Hope Connection, we learned that Dane's early neglect not only caused his brain to develop less sufficiently, but his neurotransmitters were completely out of whack. Karyn stated it much more professionally than that, but I'm not a Ph. D. student. Our son's behaviors were driven by fear and pain. When something triggered his fear or pain, the flood of neurotransmitters to his brain caused him to be completely disorganized in his thinking, and he would rage out-of-control. He was in an almost constant survival state of fight, flight, or freeze. Recognizing this helped us be more patient with him and truly understand that a meltdown was not his fault. Our job was to help him feel safe and calm down, regaining a state of rational thinking again.

We also learned that kids from "hard places" often have Sensory Processing Disorder and are highly sensitive to sights, sounds, smells, tastes, and touch. This was certainly true with Dane and explained why he could have a two-hour meltdown over a pair of socks. He couldn't stand the feel of the seam across his toes, and since he'd been very little couldn't stand to wear jeans.

He went to school every day in sweat pants or shorts. To this day, it is not uncommon to see him wearing flip flops even in the winter. Shoes are a necessity he tolerates only when he has to, like when it snows! Thankfully, that's not often in Texas.

The sensory processing piece of the puzzle also explained why our family day at Six Flags over Texas was a nightmare for him. He flipped out in that chaotic environment of sensory overload, and we ended up furious at him for ruining our day by being so aggressive and out-of-control that we had to leave. It now made sense why all stimulating environments were problematic for Dane, even something as simple as grocery stores. Hindsight is twenty-twenty, but I felt guilty that I hadn't understood all of this earlier. I also felt awful for Megan that it was so difficult, actually impossible, to do normal family things together.

It seemed like the more we learned about Dane's problems, the more there was to learn. I continued to read, research, and try new ways of managing things at home. We counseled with a therapist who had expertise with children who had come from backgrounds of neglect and abandonment. Alan and I attended a conference on Sensory Processing Disorder by Carol Kranowitz to learn more about ways to help our son. I highly recommend her book, *The Out-of-Sync Child*, and parents can learn of her website in the resource list.

Armed with new tools and a new way of looking at behaviors, we attempted to keep our family sane and moving forward. We had now accepted that our precious little boy had serious, lifelong issues, and my prayers were more about giving us strength and wisdom to get through each day rather than for a miracle for Dane. I was pretty tired of the silence and figured if God had intended to answer that prayer, he'd have done so by then. I was rather mad at him, but tried to comfort myself with the trite answers I'd heard like, "Some things we just won't understand this side of heaven." I still trusted him somewhat, I suppose, but certainly didn't like his timetable.

I thought back on that day I sang to my new son in Romania and remembered God telling me that he had a special purpose for this one. I wondered what that could possibly be. How can anything good come from all this, and where might Dane end up in adulthood with all these problems? What in the world did God have planned? Surely the plan wasn't just to kill me. "God, if you want to bring me home early, might I recommend the swift heart attack from the menu of exit plans?" I knew he had a sense of humor, and I was trying to hold on to mine, but *Geez!* I thanked him for Karyn and David, and we tried to apply all we were learning as well as educate anyone who worked with Dane.

We'd somehow make it through the school year and look forward to Hope Connection Camp in the summer. At least we'd get a fresh dose of Miss Karyn, aka, "The Child Whisperer," who renewed our hope and gave us the courage to not give up. Dane's days at camp gave us a little time off, and we'd enjoy some much needed time with the three of us. Each summer we'd learn more because

Karyn's ongoing research as well as the work of Dr. Cross continued to reveal more effective ways of dealing with troubled kids.

Even with our new education, most days were still difficult at best as we trudged forward, and each developmental stage in both of our kids brought new difficulties. Puberty was in full bloom around the Jones house, and believe me, it didn't smell at all like a garden!

Megan was now in middle school and her brother's volatile and unpredictable behavior was so embarrassing to her. We had always been the type of parents who never missed our kids' events, but she probably began to wish we would miss them. When we'd attend her volleyball or basketball games, it was not unusual for Dane to erupt into some kind of meltdown over the smallest thing. He was jealous of any attention that Alan and I gave Megan, so just being at her games was enough to enrage him, not to mention the overstimulating sights and sounds which were more than he could handle with his sensory issues. We'd try to calm him down, but it would usually end up that one of us had to take him out.

Getting a raging ten-year-old out of a crowded event does not go unnoticed. Sometimes we'd hear negative comments made under someone's breath. The hot-headed Italian in me would rise up inside, and I so wanted to give them a piece of my mind! Thankfully, the Holy Spirit in me trumped the hot-headed Italian on most days. I reminded myself that these folks had no understanding of the issues we were dealing with and perhaps I had at times misjudged someone's parenting. They spoke out of ignorance and I could excuse it, but it sure did hurt and humble me.

It became easier to avoid all the humiliation, so often Alan and I would take turns attending Megan's events. One of us would stay home with Dane, who then would throw a fit because he was missing Megan's volleyball game. The other would go to Megan's game, feeling guilty for leaving our spouse to deal with the outburst on the home front. This was almost worse than dealing with a meltdown in public. There were no easy answers, and it seemed like things were getting worse rather than better. Life was a series of choosing the lesser of two evils. Dane couldn't handle either option, so which would lead to the least amount of stress for the family?

My personal pain from seeing the ongoing suffering of my son and our family pulsed like an open wound. Fear began to consume me. I searched and searched for scriptures to soothe me. I found many and held on to them for dear life, but my daily management of all this was so exhausting, and I felt so defeated. Why wasn't I smart enough or strong enough or energetic enough or rich enough or *something* enough to find the right answers for my son?

Alan and I were growing increasingly farther apart. He had no clue what to do, and I resented him for not working harder to help me. I guessed I should be thankful he hadn't left me, because so many fathers of troubled kids bail. We knew of several marriages that had ended in divorce over children similar to Dane. We were trying hard to keep our family together and were committed to a Christ-centered marriage, but how do you have time to nurture that relationship in the midst of all this?

Both of us were so worried about Megan, and I felt such guilt that I didn't have enough time to spend with her. I remember bawling my eyes out one day to my sweet friend, Katty, who wisely said, "If God allowed all this in your lives, he certainly allowed it in hers as well. He'll use it for her good somehow and for his purpose, Deb." I knew she was right, but the words were hard to make sense of at that point in the journey. About all I could say was, "Lord, please do something!"

I spent mother-daughter time away from the house with Megan, such as lunch outings, shopping days, and little weekend trips, but home was a place where Megan spent more and more time alone, locked in her room. Who could blame her? But it broke my heart. There wasn't enough of Mom to go around, and it felt like she got the short end of the stick which she certainly didn't deserve.

By the time Megan was fourteen and Dane was eleven, the future for our family looked very hopeless. Dane was getting too big to safely restrain when he'd erupt into a violent rage. I was certified in Crisis Prevention Intervention through my position as a Special Education teacher, but Dane was very strong and hard to manage. I was emotionally fried and didn't know how I'd find the strength to live this way much longer. Alan was spent and couldn't deal with Dane's behaviors without losing his cool and yelling, which only made things worse. I certainly wasn't a saint and could end up yelling too at times, but Alan's fuse was shorter than mine. I'd end up furious with him for not handling things better, and Megan dreamed of what her life would have been like as an only child.

How much could one family take? What would be our breaking point? We didn't know what that would look like, but we knew it wouldn't be pretty. Would we end up in divorce court? Would Dane become part of the juvenile system? Would one of us get injured? Would an MS attack wipe me out? Would I somehow lose my daughter?

Hope was fading in spite of all the interventions we had tried to help Dane.

Chapter 6

· · · · · · · · · ·

The Breaking Point

I had known for months that we couldn't go on much longer. We had gained a lot of knowledge about troubled kids, but we didn't have the stamina to meet all of Dane's needs and deal with his constant meltdowns while also trying to work, raise a teenager, and go on with everyday normal life.

One Sunday afternoon Megan just snapped. Her fears erupted into anger, and she unleashed all she'd been holding in for years. She was crying and yelling, "How are we going to go on like this? What are you going to do when Dane gets too big to restrain? What if one of us gets hurt? Mom, what if your MS comes back because of all the stress and you end up in a wheelchair? I'm so sick of being embarrassed by him. And what happens when you die? Do I get stuck with all this? I want him out of here! It's him or me!"

My baby girl was throwing out questions for which I had no answers. I had secretly thought of all of them as well, but she put words to my silent fears. It was time to do something to give all of us some sort of relief, but I had no idea what that was. I didn't know for sure what she meant by "It's him or me!" and I was afraid to find out.

We made an appointment with the counselor who had been helping us with Dane. She specialized in children who were diagnosed as Reactive Attachment Disorder, and we'd spent many hours with Dane raging in her office. This time the focus was on Megan. The counselor agreed with every point Megan made about how impossible it was to live this way any longer. I had been in this struggle long enough to know there would be no easy answers. I knew we had to do something drastic, but the thought of removing him from our home ripped my guts out.

The counselor met with Alan and me privately at the end of our session with Megan. She said we were going to "sink the whole ship trying to save the one." She suggested we begin the process of moving Dane to some sort of residential treatment center. She complimented us for trying everything known to man to try to help our son and praised our efforts saying we had hung in there more than most would have. She thought that Dane would even be happier outside our home because it was the intimacy that he couldn't handle. Her recommendation was to begin with weekend respite, but then proceed to full-time placement for him and expect that he'd never be able to live with us again.

I was numb as we left her office. How could we make this decision, but how could we not? I knew we had nothing left to give Dane, and we now had two children with some serious issues. Megan felt like she'd been robbed of her parents for ten years, and we had to help her. I could not believe we were in a position of having to decide which child to save. I pleaded, "God, why can't we save them both? Please show us a way to help both of our kids!"

The next day I stayed home from work because of my overwhelming grief. I wailed in pain for hours. I couldn't believe it had come to this. How could we tell our friends that had prayed for us all those years? How could we tell Dane's teachers that had tried so hard to help him? Who would understand why we were sending our son away?

How could we tell Dane? We'd always promised him that we'd love him no matter how he behaved and would never give up on him. How could we give up now? He was eleven, but he was more like a five-year-old in so many ways. I couldn't imagine my little boy being cared for by someone else, and I knew he wouldn't understand. Would he be scared? Would he think we didn't love him anymore? How do you tell your young child he'll still be able to visit on holidays? He's still part of the family; he just doesn't live here anymore. My heart felt like it would rupture. I cried all day alone and cried some more when my family got home.

"I give. I'm defeated," I whispered to God. The battle I'd fought for so long was over. There were no more answers to find.

Late that afternoon, I called Theresa. She understood me better than anyone. I must have left my weight in mascara on her shoulders over the past ten years. This time I was beyond a basket case. I remember walking around to the front side of the house in my pajamas just sobbing into the phone. Guess at that point I didn't care what the neighbors thought. I didn't want Dane to hear me crying so I'd sneaked outside leaving Alan in charge. I hoped a three-hour meltdown wouldn't be waiting for me when I came back in, as I had no strength left. So many times I'd said that I didn't have time for the nervous breakdown I deserved.

I hid behind the air conditioner unit, bawling my eyes out as my body curled into a fetal position. I remember my little dog, Buddy, hanging out with me as I poured out my wounded soul to the only person who could even begin to grasp what I was feeling. There were no words that could comfort me, but Theresa was there. Theresa was always there.

The days that followed were dark and empty. I felt like I was in a bad dream and longed for someone to wake me. My mourning felt comparable to a death, only we were participants in the decision to send him away. Guilt consumed me. I wrestled to find some sort of peace by listening to praise music which had always soothed me. One of my favorite songs at that time was "Call on Jesus" by Nicole C Mullens. It was like she'd written those words for me:

If you're tired and scared of the madness around you
If you can't find the strength to carry on
 When you call on Jesus,
All things are possible
You can mount on wings like eagles and soar (August 28, 2001, *Talk About It* album)

On this particular day, I was inconsolable. I played the song and in my grief I became enraged. I screamed at the God I loved. "Yeah, you can call on Jesus and he'll say no. That's all I ever seem to hear from you, God, is NO, NO, NO! Why won't you heal my son, anyway? It's not like I'm asking for some selfish request like a fancy car in the driveway. Don't you want him to be whole? I've prayed to you, I've trusted you, I've begged you. I've digested every verse I can find searching for answers. I don't understand why I have to send him away now after all we've gone through. Where are you? Is this your plan, for me to feel abandoned too, just like Dane? Am I supposed to be learning some big lesson here? I think I've had enough character building, and I just don't get it! I feel as out-of-control as Dane right now. Who are you??? Just like he asks me, I'm asking you! God, are you nice or mean?"

Silence. Silence that hurt.

I didn't hear any immediate answer or gain some huge revelation, so I began the paperwork for a facility where Dane could go for weekend respite. I was nauseated as I filled it out. More questions about all his inappropriate behaviors. *UGH! Yes, he does all of the above and then some!* I was sick of questionnaires that listed everything he did wrong, but offered no solutions. How many of these had I filled out in ten years? How many thousands of dollars had we spent trying to help him? I certainly wasn't going to add it up because I didn't want to know.

Had any of it really helped? Was sending him away the answer? I couldn't imagine that he would get better with people who didn't love him like we did. I guessed we'd at least have a little rest and could have some sort of normal family life, but how could we be a family without our son?

Within a week of my temper tantrum with God, I was lying on the couch exhausted from grieving so hard when the phone rang. Karyn from Hope Connection called to check on us. I'd confided in her a few days earlier about how bad things were and of our recent decision to seek placement outside of our home for Dane.

She offered to bring in a team of professionals to implement an intense home-based intervention with us as a last ditch effort to try to help Dane and save our family. It would involve keeping him within arm's reach during all waking hours and working solely on getting his behaviors under control and building attachment that he'd missed the first year of life. I would need to take a leave of absence from my job, and Dane would be placed on homebound instruction for a few months depending on how quickly he progressed. Karyn would be there periodically to support and coach us during the beginning weeks. All of this would be at no cost to our family, but there was a catch, a big one!

A major television network would be taping our progress for the duration of the home intervention and the story would then air on prime time TV.

Are you nuts? I wanted to blurt out. There was no way I was going to allow any of this on TV. No one could begin to understand the complex issues involved in our child's problems. Heck, we didn't even understand it all, and we were living it. I could only imagine how embarrassing and painful all this already was for Megan, and I surely wasn't going to hurt her further. Plus, Alan and I were teachers in our small community. The wrong slant on this story could make us look like idiots who didn't know anything about parenting and children. No way!

I politely told her that I would have to decline. She asked that I at least meet the producer and talk it over with her. I said that wouldn't be necessary. Karyn in her sweet, persuasive way quietly said, "Well, just pray about it." I asked when she needed an answer, and she gently replied, "When you have one."

I thought, *Okay, I'll pray about it. But God better tell me no because there is no way in hell I'm doing that!* I was well-acquainted with hearing no from him, so why stop now? I talked it over with Alan who agreed that it was way too risky. When I mentioned it to Megan, she begged, "No, Mom! No, Mom! Please don't ever let any of this be put on TV."

My stomach churned for weeks. I avoided praying about it because surely God wouldn't put us through this kind of humiliation. But my mind couldn't help but wonder if this intense home-based intervention might be the one thing we hadn't tried and could make a significant difference in Dane's behavior and help him connect to us. I reasoned, rationalized, and asked for advice from others. Finally, I threw up a quick prayer with a fleece. "God, if you want us to do this I need an angel-with-a-note kind of answer. I'm even going to tell you what I want that to be. If we're supposed to do this, I need Megan to come on board. I can't hurt her anymore."

I breathed a sigh of relief because I was certain that Megan would never agree to subjecting our family to cameras in our home, capturing the lowest moments with her little brother. She had heard "a temporary sacrifice for a long-term goal" too many times before. I couldn't imagine it either, even though I was interested in learning more about this intervention. It was true that many families could be helped if it was a success, but what if it wasn't? We'd be worse off than before and still end up having to send Dane away.

Not long after my angel-with-a-note prayer, Megan came to me one day and said, "Mom, if these people might really have answers that could help Dane, I guess having your face on TV is a small price to pay. I think you should call Karyn."

Tears still stream down my face when I think about that moment. What a brave young lady to risk so much after all she'd already suffered in our family life. I guess she hadn't totally given up on Dane after all.

A mixture of hope and dread came over me as I picked up the phone.

Chapter 7

· · · · · · · · · ·

Intervention at Home

W e had always said that some of Dane's behaviors were not that abnormal, but it was the frequency, intensity, and duration that made them abnormal. As the team entered our home, it was clear that *frequency, intensity, and duration* were coming our way. We would devote every waking minute of each day to stopping the violence, meeting his needs, connecting, and correcting his thinking and maladaptive behaviors.

Karyn had taught us so much about brain development, attachment, neurochemistry, and sensory processing during our time at Hope Connection. We had tried to apply what we'd learned in the context of our everyday lives, but what Dane needed was an intense time of nurture, structure, and training that could only be done at home. Dane still needed what he'd missed during those critical months of early brain development while he was in the orphanage. We as parents needed to learn how to "redo" infancy with a raging eleven-year-old.

We had learned from Karyn in scientific terms that "recovery of function recapitulates the development of function." While that might not make you all warm and fuzzy inside, what it means is that if you need to relearn something, you'll relearn it exactly like you did the first time. For instance, if you lose language skills from having a stroke and must relearn to talk, you'll learn exactly like you did when you were a baby.

Dane's brain needed the constant mentoring that an adoring mother gives a newborn in order to develop. He needed sensory input that his brain didn't get lying alone in a wet crib in an orphanage. He needed his fears to be disarmed and to feel safe so that his neurotransmitters could function better. And he needed to learn how to trust, which happens in the first year of life when an infant's needs are continually met by a loving caregiver. He needed to learn to accept "no" which is typically learned in the second year of life.

Was a child's brain something we could wipe clean like a slate and reprogram? Could he really regain what he missed in the first months of life and then progress forward?

Karyn brought us several professionals to help us on our journey: a neuropsychologist who did a battery of neurological tests to determine where Dane was functioning cognitively and developmentally as well as taught us how to structure our day and stop the violence; an occupational therapist who did a sensory processing profile and taught us sensory activities we could do at home; a counselor who helped us deal with our own unresolved issues as well as correct our thinking and expectations; and Dr. David Cross, her trusted colleague from Hope Connection who offered devoted friendship to Dane and a strong shoulder to lean on for his hurting dad. In addition, Dane had a homebound instructor from our local school district to meet his educational needs. Talk about, "It takes a village!"

I'm not sure if you can imagine this many professionals really working in your home, but it felt like we were now operating our own personal psych ward. If that wasn't challenging enough, there was the whole taping issue. We had hidden cameras in the prominent areas of our home, scheduled camera crews for major taping days, and frequent visits from the producer. I was taught how to tape some of the chaos on a handheld camera from the studio to show Dane's behaviors and progress. We surely hoped there would be progress. I was relying on the experts, for I believed they were divinely appointed and finally an answer to my prayers. Surely God wouldn't have brought us this far to let us fail and be publicly humiliated. I desperately hoped not. *God, I believe that this is the answer to my angel-with-a-note prayer. If it's not, please tell me now.*

Three days after Christmas, which happened to be my birthday, was our first day of parent training in our home. *Happy Birthday, Debbie!* Little did I know, this would turn out to be one of the greatest gifts God had ever given me . . . .

Our first full day at home on the new intervention—with a house full of professionals—involved laying the groundwork for Dane. They would soon leave, and I would carry out all we'd learned with Alan to help relieve me on nights and weekends. It was explained to Dane that all these behaviors were interfering with his relationships and ruining his life. He was headed for serious trouble if we didn't help him, so for now we were going to focus completely on family and not things. This meant we had to remove the distractions for a period of time. No TV, no video games, no computer, no time with friends, no toys or games unless they were used in parent directed times of structured play. His face sank as we told him all of this was going away for a while. We reassured him that it wasn't punishment, but that it was to help him learn that our family relationships were more important than all this "stuff."

We explained to him that Mom and Dad were in charge and that he needed to ask permission for everything. And I mean everything. This sounds almost dictatorial, but we as parents had to realize that Dane was not truly dependent on us and didn't know how to trust us even though he was dearly loved. That's why he was such a control freak. Without the ability to trust others, he had to be in control at all times. An important truth in developmental psychology is that dependence must precede independence. If we ever wanted him to reach any level of independence, he was going to have to experience true dependence on his parents. He had to learn to trust us and that would develop through having his needs met, literally thousands of times in the months to come.

Babies depend on their parents for everything—food, warmth, safety, touch, nurture, comfort, and love. Dane had missed this important part of development which is vital to healthy attachment as well as brain development, neurochemistry, and sensory processing. We also learned that most children who have experienced early harm are unable to express their needs. They've in a sense lost their voice. We had to teach Dane to "use his words" to get what he needed or wanted. Now, rather than head to the kitchen and grab a snack, he had to ask permission, and then Dad or I would go prepare it for him or with him. He had to verbalize his need to get some exercise, go outside, or get a drink, and a parent was right there within arm's distance during all waking hours.

Did that register? Alan or I were within about three feet of Dane at all times. I can just feel the parents reacting to this as I write. Three feet? How would I ever get anything done? Well, I didn't get much done. Remember, we were about to lose our son. This was a last-ditch effort to keep him at home. If he didn't connect to us, develop trust, and learn to use words instead of violence to get his needs met, he wasn't going to make it in our family. I said earlier that I took a leave of absence from my job, but what I really did was take a leave of absence from my life.

The *intensity, frequency, and duration* needed to bring this child back online left little room for anything else. Karyn and David call this "investment parenting." I didn't take phone calls, I didn't go to church, I dropped out of ladies' Bible study, I didn't work, I didn't go out with friends, and any housekeeping and cooking were done with Dane right beside me. I did occasionally call to report to Theresa that I was indeed still alive, and she would relay it to our other friends. Not all of them understood, but I knew I had to give it my all or my family would never survive.

With the guidance of our intervention team, we mapped out the behaviors that were most interfering with his life and our family. We wrote out goals on a poster board, along with photographs of him to help him visualize and grasp what we were teaching. For instance, we had a picture of Dane with a pleasant facial expression and contrasted it with a picture of his "mean" face. Dane was very concrete and literal in his thinking so we made everything as visual as possible to help him understand. This poster became like a curriculum for teaching him new ways of thinking and behaving. We went over it morning, afternoon, evening, and at bedtime.

Dane's neurological testing revealed that he had significant delays in language development, so we simplified our language and used as few words as possible, especially when behaviors were deteriorating. We learned that at this point the child is not able to process much information and is functioning in the lower, more primitive regions of the brain. During a meltdown, he was literally in a survival state of fight, flight, or freeze. So as parents, we had to use few words and control our tone of voice so as to not escalate his fear-based survival responses. The goal was to stay connected and help him feel safe. "Felt safety" was an important concept for us to learn as parents. While we knew Dane was safe in our home, he didn't always know it or feel safe. We had to realize that due to his early neglect and harm, his brain was hard-wired to sense any hint of threat. Hypervigilance is common in children from "hard places." The slightest facial expression showing disapproval or anger would cause Dane to overreact. Any misunderstanding of humor due to his limited cognitive functioning would cause him to feel rejected and not safe. We had to become like detectives, not only watching out for things in his environment that might set him off, but watching our own actions, words, and nonverbal messages that could arouse fear and feelings of insecurity.

Throughout each day, we would work on developing his vocabulary and required him to speak in complete sentences to strengthen his language skills as well as reinforce the behavioral concepts he needed to learn. We'd ask him, "Who's in charge, Dane?" He'd answer, "Mom and Dad." Then we'd remind him, "Say it in a whole sentence" to which he'd reply, "My mom and dad are in charge." We'd probe a little further, "Some of the time or all of the time?" He'd say, "All of the time." A quick reminder about the whole sentence, and he'd recite, "My mom and dad are in charge all the time."

Many times he couldn't construct his own complete sentence so we'd have to model it for him and have him repeat it back to us. Looking back, it felt like we said this mantra and many other behavioral scripts about a million times. It took so much repetition for Dane to learn due to his limited cognitive processing from the early insult of alcohol and lead toxicity.

We not only discussed each goal, we role-played and practiced them. We played games like "Wrong Way/ Right Way" to give him the many repetitions it took for learning to take place and new neural connections to be made. This was done when he was in a calm state, not when needing correction or acting out in defiance. He was literally creating new neural pathways and motor memory in his brain. We practiced the most on the areas that needed the most work.

For example, I'd say, "Show me the wrong way to behave when I tell you it's time to brush your teeth." He'd yell "No!" and throw a fit on the floor. Then I'd say, "Now show me the right way," and he'd respond with "Okay, Mom," and he'd head to the bathroom with a grin and grab his toothbrush. Then we'd reverse roles and play again. "Now you are the parent and I'll be the child," at which time I'd try to mimic as closely as I could the way Dane typically behaved, but not in a way that looked like I was making fun of him or putting him down.

Some days it took hours just to gain compliance. We'd end up in a meltdown because he didn't want to go over his goal poster, brush his teeth, or get dressed for the day. Once he was back on track, we'd go back and start our practice again until he got it right. Needless to say, he had really clean teeth in those days!

The occupational therapist taught us to include some type of sensory activity every two hours. Dane and I often went bike riding together, jumped on the trampoline, played basketball, and went for walks. On bad weather days, we played crab walk soccer down the hall, wheelbarrow games, and various animal walks and army crawls on the floor, which provided deep sensory input that is calming to the central nervous system. We made tents in the living room, rearranging furniture and covering chairs with blankets, pretending we were camping. We danced to our favorite songs and made up lyrics to music for some of his behavioral goals. I used every trick I knew to solidify the new goals in his mind. We played a lot, but it was play with a purpose, and it was always together.

Dane loved the constant one-on-one attention, and after a few weeks it began to feel like we were recovering some of the lost years when he had been so out-of-control. As we progressed through our intervention, I was actually enjoying playing with him again. Not so long ago, we had all been so wiped out from dealing with constant behavioral issues, threats, and aggression that it was hard to find any joy in the relationship. He was often so dysregulated from overstimulation in his environment that family outings were awful, but in the safety of our home with no demands on my schedule, we had all the time in the world for learning, playing, and connecting.

The days were long and exhausting. In the beginning, I couldn't even get a shower until Alan came home from work to relieve me. If I went to the bathroom, Dane stood right outside the door, and I talked to him the whole time to make sure he wasn't getting into any trouble for that minute and a half. We made early bedtimes a part of our schedule and if it had been a really bad day, he went to bed even earlier. It was the only way I had the strength to get up and tackle it all again the next day.

Thoughts of Megan consumed my mind. She had endured so much and felt like she'd been robbed of her parents for so many years. I knew I couldn't make up for the loss, but did she understand that we were trying to help all of us and were fighting for a better tomorrow for our family? If I spent any time away from the house, it was with her. Alan would take a shift on the weekends, so I could go for mother/daughter outings. I'd try to cheer her up with shopping, lunch, and long talks; however, for the most part, it felt like she was slipping away.

She was so scared. When she agreed to have cameras invade our lives, she didn't realize how much worse things would get before they got better. She was so embarrassed that her friends would see all of this. Behind the scenes, she was praying that the network would go out of business. The producer originally wanted to involve her more in the story, but she was in too much pain for us to press her. I was grateful for a producer with a tender heart.

Many with tender hearts were bathing our family in prayer. I was mostly praying we'd have the strength to get through. I was glad that others were praying for me because my faith felt shattered. I'd given up on even knowing what to pray. At this point in my faith journey, my conversations with God went more like, "What kind of God are you? What kind of father would allow his own child to go through this much pain and suffering? I've read in James 1 about testing which produces endurance, but this much? I'm trying to teach Dane to trust me, but can I trust you? No disrespect intended, but sometimes I think you act more mentally ill than I do, not that I've had time to go get diagnosed through all of this!"

Even though I felt confused about whether God was nice or mean, Alan and I both felt God had led us to this point, and we did recognize that he was in charge. "My ways are not your ways" was certain. (Isaiah 55:8) I had always prayed for a miracle, but our answer was more in the form of an exodus. At least it was an answer.

As with most behavioral interventions, things with Dane got worse before they got better. I tried to silence the doubts that were barking in my head. One of my favorite memory verses had been put to the test. "And we know that God causes all things to work together for good to those who love God, to those who are called according to His purpose." Romans 8:28. *God, I can't understand your purpose in all this, but I'm trying to believe. I'm trying to hold on to your truth.*

I had to depend on God for every ounce of strength to get through those months. I felt bad that I'd been so mad at him, but knew he understood. I was beginning to understand that he truly "gets me" no matter what and just like I would never give up on Dane, he would never give up on me. I thought about my spiritual adoption and began to definitely see God as my adopted daddy, my Abba Father. Parents of troubled kids know how to love their kids regardless of their behavior, and I was comforted by knowing how much he loved me no matter how I behaved. I was experiencing a bit of "felt safety" myself and was grateful to sense his presence and feel connected to him like never before.

One day I had a huge revelation as I was attempting to head off another power struggle with my mantra, "Who's in charge, Dane?" It felt as if God was saying, "Who's in charge, Debbie?" I shot up a quick, "You are, God." It even seemed like I heard in my head, "Some of the time or all of the time? Whole sentence!" I cracked myself up as I replied, "God, you are in charge all of the time." Was he trying to teach me that trusting in him meant that dependence had to come first just like we were teaching Dane to depend on us? *Okay God, your way, not my way. I'm yours, and I'm depending on you for every step of this difficult journey.*

As Alan and I worked intensely with Dane, he fought hard to maintain control. It was so hard for him to trust that we truly would take care of him and that he didn't have to get his way or fight us to be safe. Some of the meltdowns were over such ridiculous stuff like what shirt to wear, but it was really a battle of who was in charge. His little brain was hard-wired to think he had to be in charge and that often meant a complete three-hour meltdown with raging, screaming, threatening, hitting, and kicking. It's not the intent of this book to train you in how to safely stop violence, so please check with your own state for safe methods and best practices.

Once Dane was settled enough to self-regulate, I'd cradle him like a baby (yes, his legs were almost as long as mine). I'd look deeply into his eyes while talking gently to him to correct his thinking about what just happened and how to prevent it next time using words to ask for what he needed. It always astounded me that the same child who was cussing, screaming, and threatening to kill me could afterwards melt back into my arms and capture my heart when I saw that "real boy" within all that chaos. I always knew he was in there!

We used the term "real boy" with him as we'd seen Karyn model at Hope Connection. Sometimes we could head off a would-be-meltdown by saying, "Dane, show me that real boy and use your words to tell me what you need." We were all fighting for that real child within who loved his family and had a deep desire to be connected. And that "real boy" would steal my heart every time in such a way that I could barely stop the tears.

I cried so much during those days. It was so hard. I felt so alone. It was up and down. It was progress, then regress. It was three steps forward, two steps back. Tears of sadness, tears of joy. Times of doubt, moments of faith. But as a hint of spring was beginning to awaken, it started to feel like there was hope for brighter days ahead.

Chapter 8

· · · · · · · · · ·

Hope, Sunshine, Rainbows

February was so rough that at one point, I hit the power button on the hidden camera as I roared at Alan, "Forget the cameras! We just gotta get through this." It took everything I had just to make it through each day. It was so painful and exhausting that I didn't have the strength to video all the drama in my home to try to help others. I didn't know at that point if we were going to make it as a family and if this child could be saved, much less whether my marriage could survive all of this. I had shared all the tears that I was willing to share.

About this time in the program, Alan checked out emotionally. He wasn't threatening to leave or anything, he was just oblivious to what he was supposed to be doing. One evening Dane was in a complete screaming, raging meltdown which I was handling alone, our little dog, Buddy, was barking like crazy outside the door, and Alan was sitting on the couch reading the newspaper as if he were enjoying the solitude of a quiet study. I'm sure I nearly scared him to death when I yelled at the top of my lungs, "Could you AT LEAST let the dog in?" *Good grief! Is he in a mild coma? How can he be so clueless that I need help here?*

He just couldn't handle it anymore. I was worn to a frazzle and knew I'd never make it flying solo on this intense program. I poured out my heart to Karyn, who wisely discerned that it wasn't that Alan didn't want to help me; he couldn't. All of this chaos, mixed with so much emotional intimacy, triggered his childhood abandonment issues and personal history that were yet to be resolved. Karyn explained to me that every single member of my family was in survival mode. Each one of us was fighting for his or her very life and trying to hold on in the only way we knew how. The kicker was when she added, "And Debbie, you're the only one who gets it."

No pressure here! How in the world are we going to get through? It looks so impossible. God, you alone can heal us.

With a new compassion for Alan, I went to him following my talk with Karyn. Taking his face in both of my hands and looking into his eyes, I begged, "Honey, I know this is so hard and triggering your own pain, but please give me six months of your undivided attention. I mean fully present, really working hard together, undivided attention. If you want this to work and our family to make it, I have to have you on board."

I can honestly say that he pulled himself out of his funk and gave his family everything he had for that season of our lives. The TV stayed off, the newspapers had to wait, and Alan was right by my side during the evenings when he came home from work. I know it was mentally and physically exhausting for him. After teaching high school seniors all day, he'd come home to having to support or sometimes completely spell me so I could have the energy to get up and continue on the next day. It was the hardest thing either of us had ever endured in our lives. This school teacher can't come up with adjectives strong enough to describe the exhaustion and emotional drain we experienced, but through our dependence on God we had the strength to keep going.

There are times in life when you just have to press on. February of 2002 was one of those times. One of Dane's worst meltdowns was during that month, and it seemed to be a major turning point. Following this episode, Dane had what I later learned is called an "infantile regression." As he was cradled in my arms while we both collapsed after the exhausting battle, he seemed to be having an almost out-of-body experience.

I was holding him with my arms wrapped around his shoulders and looking into his eyes while soothing him. Suddenly, he became frightened, began crying more like a young infant, and started almost begging, "No, Mom. No, Mom. Don't put your hands around my throat!" I talked quietly to him assuring him that my arms were around his shoulders and that he was safe. He continued to say, "Don't touch my throat. Move your hands, Mom. Don't put your hands on my throat." I was so confused and didn't quite know what to do, but I just kept talking softly to him, showed him again that my hands were not near his throat, and let him know I was there and would never hurt him. He finally began to relax and in the next few minutes we both just melted into my bed with him cuddled close beside me.

After a brief rest, he popped up, returned to his "real boy" voice and in a very matter-of-fact tone said, "Ya know, I think before my birth mother took me to the orphanage, she tried to kill me." Chill bumps ran down my spine as I asked, "Why do you think that?" His light-hearted reply, "I don't know. I just do." And that was it.

I felt like my brain was rummaging through file cabinets to try to connect this new information to something I'd learned. He was just under a year old when he came home, so how could he possibly remember even if that had happened to him? We had been told that his birth mother took him to the "hospital" when he was two months old because he was sick, and she couldn't care for him. Then she just never went back. I use the word hospital loosely because the hospitals we saw were no different than orphanages. An institution that cared for the young infants was supposedly a hospital, but babies were literally housed there until they were about a year old and then moved to orphanages. It seemed to us like the only difference was the age of the children that were warehoused.

This whole infantile regression scene happened just before Karyn was to arrive at our home for a visit. I could not wait to see what she thought about all this. When I described what had happened and what Dane said about his birth mother trying to kill him, Karyn said she wouldn't be at all surprised if that had actually happened.

"The body never forgets, and we've heard spontaneous stories very similar to this from numerous other children," she said. "Even though he may not be able to recall what happened at a conscious level, he probably has some sense of what happened to him. It was not uncommon for mothers to try to kill their children rather than resort to leaving them in orphanages." She encouraged me to never discount anything he said, but just comfort him through it and allow him to tell his story.

My heart ached. What trauma had my son suffered in his first weeks of life? We'd never know for sure, but we knew it was worse than we'd previously imagined. Poor thing. No wonder he was such a mess for so many years. I so wished I could take it all away, but knew he had to grieve the loss to heal and move forward with any kind of normalcy.

Alan and I continued to reassure him that we would never give up on him and would love him always. As we shaped his behaviors through much practice and taught him with praise and guidance, we celebrated that he was learning to use his words rather than behaviors to get his needs met. Our precious little boy was becoming more secure and finally beginning to trust us. I often felt like I was steering an out-of-control locomotive, and I had to be keenly aware of what might set him off so I could get him back on the track. I was deliberate about setting him up to succeed and setting manageable goals that would typically be reasonable for a much younger child. The intense time alone with him helped me to be so in tune with him that my predicting and steering improved and his behavior improvements followed.

By March, I was ready to share with others again and was soon crying into the camera. Dane had made such significant gains that we allowed him to invite over a friend. This was his first play date with a friend in three months, and he did so great that I just became a blubbering puddle. This was a moment I wanted the world to see, so I grabbed the handheld camera and poured out my heart. "Twenty-two days without a meltdown! Do you get this? Can you get this? We're talking twenty-two days! My child has been playing for over an hour, and I'm sittin' here bawling with the video camera. And I know that seems crazy to be crying because your kid's playing, but he couldn't do this before."

That was the day it really sunk in with me that he was going to get better. He'd come so far in three months that I knew that I knew that I knew he was going to get better!

Hope.

We finally had hope for a better tomorrow. We knew it wouldn't all be easy and he definitely still had some bad days, but we knew what to do and had a track to run on. We knew to look for the fear and pain that lay beneath the meltdown. We knew how to see it coming and remind him to take a deep breath and use his words. We no longer feared for his future and that of the whole family.

I stayed home from work a few more weeks to solidify the gains he had made and continue to reinforce appropriate behaviors. We gradually introduced more privileges and responsibility as he continued to improve. We'd raise the bar just a little when it was time to set new expectations. Sometimes we misjudged and had to regroup, but we never again lost all hope.

Within six months from our start date, Dane was smiling more than we'd ever seen. There was a peace and contentment about him that I don't think he'd ever known.

He now knew we'd never give up. We now knew we'd never give up. And we all now knew God would never give up on us.

I felt like God had just reached down and rescued our family. My thoughts went back to that bittersweet first day of being his legal mother in a humble flat in Romania. *Why you? Why do you get to be plucked out of here?* Then I began to wonder . . . why us? Why did we get to have this help when there are thousands of families suffering with similar issues? I didn't know and I don't fully know now, except that God had a plan. It certainly wasn't the path I would have chosen, but it was a plan nonetheless. I was grateful to be a part of it and grateful that Dane was my son. Maybe God just knew a loud-mouthed, passionate Italian like me would have to tell my story.

If you are a parent on a difficult journey, I so desperately want you to know that things can get better. It's not easy, but it is worth it to invest in the life of a child. At the time we began our home intervention, we believed it was a "pay now or pay severely later" situation and we are so glad that on December 28, we chose "pay now." Children with wounds can heal, and parents with broken hearts can teach them how to trust and not be afraid. Spring does follow a long, cold winter and the sun comes out after the darkness.

In our final interview, eight months after allowing the network into our home, the correspondent asked us what it felt like to see such progress in a short time. With eyes twinkling, Alan answered, "Hope, sunshine, rainbows!"

Chapter 9

. . . .

Brighter Days

M y leave of absence from life was coming to a close. We started with baby steps like eating out, having the grandparents over, and taking the family back to church. The three-foot rule was eased up gradually, and Dane was able to spend time alone or with friends as long as his behavior was okay. If he regressed, he went back to close proximity with more rehearsal and practice. He did have a few more meltdowns, but continued to have longer stretches between episodes and they were shorter in duration. We now had a system in place and felt like we had a track to run on. We as parents changed as much or more than he did. We now knew that if he was losing control, something had triggered his fear or pain. Rather than assigning heavy consequences for misbehavior, we helped him figure out what he was afraid of and how we could help him.

Alan and I felt so blessed that our family had been given a second chance. We would have done anything to keep our family together, and were so grateful to all who had helped us. We had gone from hopelessness to feeling like we had literally been rescued by God. Before our home-based intervention, Dane was misbehaving about 90 percent of the time, and we'd see the "real Dane" about 10 percent of the time. Six months later, those numbers had been reversed. Dane was behaving appropriately about 90 percent of the time. The 10 percent of the time that he acted up could still be rough, but it was manageable now. We weren't so worn out and emotionally exhausted that we couldn't handle it.

Dane went back to school, I returned to work, and we continued to set new goals and practice appropriate behaviors. The staff at Dane's elementary school was very willing to make the necessary accommodations to complement the work we were doing with him at home. By middle school, Dane was controlling himself quite well at school, and my heart no longer skipped a beat when I'd see the school's phone number on my caller ID.

Sometimes it felt like Dane regressed to progress. At each major developmental milestone he'd have a rough time where his behaviors deteriorated, such as when he went from elementary to middle school. Transitions are so difficult for children from "hard places" and they were still difficult for Dane due to his learning disabilities and hypervigilance, so we role-played and rehearsed before each new transition in his life. We now recognized that during those times he needed big doses of connecting with Mom and Dad.

His chronological age was pushing him to be more independent, but we knew his emotional needs were more like that of a toddler. Sometimes it felt like I was in a push-pull relationship with Dane. He needed me close to feel safe, but was trying so hard to be the cool middle school kid—like the time he went to his first school dance. Sending a child with his background and issues to an event where even the popular kids have sweaty palms was scary. We tried so hard to never put him in a situation where he'd surely fail, but what a dilemma!

The environment alone had enough sensory stimulation to send him over the edge—a crowded cafeteria, loud music, flashing lights, and heavily perfumed girls just to name a few! Next there were numerous opportunities to trigger his abandonment issues—his friend, Joseph, getting to dance while he stands alone, pubescent girls giggling in secret, and heaven forbid if he got up the nerve to ask one of them to dance and she said no! This much potential rejection in a sensory nightmare was so risky, but he was determined to go. I'm not sure whose neurotransmitters were more off the charts that whole week, Dane's or mine? I was doing my deep breathing and self-talk to get myself through as well.

Pre-teaching was our norm, so we talked about and role-played every possible scenario, including how to dance. I halfway thought he'd chicken out, but when it came time for the dance he was still all for it. He was nervous about going in alone, but didn't really want me there either. This almost led to a meltdown, but we steered him through and he kept his cool. Having learned from Karyn how to negotiate a compromise, he decided to have me go in and stand with him in line to buy his ticket and help with any money issues. Then I was to head to the car before he went into the school cafeteria. I felt like I was strategizing a war just to get him through this big event. I wondered how many other parents just had to deal with buying their kid a new outfit! *Oh well, that's not my world.*

We got to the school, and I was soon kicking myself that we hadn't arrived earlier. How did I miss that preparation? Waiting in long lines was definitely not one of his strengths. Somehow we made it through the ticket line even though he was muttering rude comments to me under his breath. Thankfully, it was loud in there, so I pretended not to hear his grumbles and just kept reassuring him that he was going to have fun. I knew he didn't mean anything he said, but was so scared that he reverted to his old ways of blaming and maintaining control. I actually admired him for having the courage to even go and smiled when I thought about how a couple of years earlier we could barely get through a trip to the grocery store.

If he pulls this off, it will be a huge accomplishment for him and so good for his self-esteem. I tried not to let my mind wander to all the "what-ifs" should this night go south. A huge meltdown in front of all these middle schoolers would set him back for months and take a lot of repair on our part. *Please, Lord, help him hold it together.*

With ticket in hand, Dane gave me the signal that it was time for me to go. I headed to the car, praying with every step. That three-hour dance had to be one of the longest nights of my life. The phone didn't ring, so at least I knew he hadn't gotten into big trouble with the principal. But what might he unload when he got home if he'd gotten his feelings hurt? I was bracing myself for what could have been a huge meltdown.

Finally it was time to go pick him up. Alan went with me for backup, just in case . . . . As we watched the teens pouring out of the building, here came our "real boy" with a grin as big as Texas and strutting a little prouder than he'd gone in. *Thank You, God!*

Dane said he had a great time and even danced with a girl. Whew! I poured on the praise about what a huge victory this was for him. What a great kid! I was so proud and once again thanking God for how far Dane had come. I was acting like he'd just won an Olympic medal.

This was huge for him and huge for our family. I kept feeling more hope as he continued to progress. If he had come this far, he could progress more. Maybe he would have a better life than we'd anticipated. For years we'd taught him that God had a plan for him, and we often reminded him of his life verse. "'For I know the plans I have for you,' declares the Lord, 'plans for welfare and not for calamity, to give you a future and a hope'" (Jeremiah 29:11).

During middle school it became evident that Dane was quite a talented runner. Academics were definitely not his strength so it was great for him to have an area in which he excelled. He participated on the track team for a short time, but the meets were late in the evening and that was when Dane had the most trouble with self-regulation, so it didn't work out. He was just too emotionally worn out late in the day to manage that much pressure and stress.

By high school he had improved so much that we decided to give it a try again. High school meets were in the morning and that gave him better odds at success. Being on the team was a great time in Dane's life. He did quite well on both the cross-country team as well as the track and field team in the spring. His coach was a wonderful man who gave Dane the extra encouragement he needed. One way that God was consistent in Dane's life was that he always provided someone who understood and wanted to help him. We felt so blessed.

By Dane's sophomore year, he had earned his letter jacket. Alan was teaching at Dane's high school and loved to brag to his students about all his son had accomplished in track. Dane loved the approval from the other kids, and we were thrilled that after all his struggles, he was earning medals and trophies. He even won first place in the district cross-country meet and was proud to sport his gold medal. With each victory, Alan and I would be on the sidelines welling up with tears. We were proud that he was winning, but secretly thinking, *if all these people only knew how far this kid has come!* He is able to control himself. He is able to reach goals. He is able to express his needs. He is able to wait. He is able to handle crowds. He is able to handle competition. He is able to handle defeat. He is able . . . .

When you have a child with severe disabilities, it seems you spend much time focusing on what he is unable to do. It was so great to see that Dane is able! And that my God is "able to do exceeding abundantly beyond all that we ask or think, according to the power that works within us" (Ephesians 3:20).

At the time of this writing, Dane has far exceeded what our expectations were for a child with the early insult of alcohol and lead toxicity as well as abandonment, neglect, and trauma. Ten years post-home intervention, Dane is twenty-one years of age and has reached a level of independence we never dreamed possible. Dane lives in his own apartment near our home and works in grounds and maintenance there. He cares for his loyal dog, Hershey. He is active in our church and has relationships there. He is connected to his family and knows he is loved. He has handled some big losses and disappointments with courage, and he uses his words to get his needs met. Life is still not always easy for him due to his early harm and cognitive impairments, but he is learning to trust God and operate in faith rather than fear.

Our family has overcome tremendous obstacles and all the glory goes to God. Alan and I faced our own demons from our past and are continuing to build the marriage we always dreamed of. Megan has grown into an amazing young woman with strength, courage, brilliance, and a hilarious sense of humor. She had a tough character-building course growing up, but she hung in there with us and as she once wrote in the last line of her childhood poem, "And I am the Band-Aid that sticks with them all." Her parents could not be more proud!

Medicine Chest Poem

by Megan Jones, age 11

My family lives in a medicine chest.
My father is the soap,
That washes away my worries.
My mother is the Advil,
That takes away my pain.
My brother is the cough syrup,
That irritates me always, but means well.
My dog is the toothpaste,
That freshens up my day.
My cat is the hot pad,
That is always mad.
And I am the Band-Aid,
That sticks with them all.

Dane recently had the opportunity to speak to a group of adoptive parents at TCU's Hope Connection Camp. I thought he'd talk about what it felt like to have so much anger and fear as a young child and maybe share about our behavior intervention we did at home. I steered him that direction, but much to my surprise, he sounded more like a little evangelist as he encouraged those parents. He seemed to reach right into their souls as he pleaded, "Don't ever give up on your child. My parents never gave up on me and don't ever give up! There's a real boy or a real girl in there and God has a plan for them. God has a special purpose." Then he quoted his memory verse from Jeremiah 29:11. There wasn't a dry eye in the room, and I don't think I've ever heard anything quite so powerful. God certainly can use the weak to lead the strong. If you were to meet Dane today, he'd probably say, "Has my mom told you my story? Ya know—I'm a miracle!"

Chapter 10

· · · · · · · · · · ·

Trusting My Abba Father

If you were to meet me today, I'd also probably say, "Ya know—I'm a miracle!"

The four months I spent alone at home with Dane were life-changing for me. I heard God more clearly than I had in all the thirty plus years since my childhood salvation when I'd prayed to receive Christ. I didn't hear him audibly, but I sensed his presence in a way that is hard to describe and that is so precious to me. There would be thoughts in my head that didn't sound like me, but sounded like him and they sounded like an adoptive daddy. He was truly my only hope and quite often the only one I had to talk to until Alan came home from work during those long and tiresome days.

I often sensed deep in my spirit as I'd pour out my guts to him about how much I loved Dane and wanted to help him know and understand my love no matter what his issues were, that God was saying, "And that's how I love you, Deb. I'll never give up on you. I have a plan for you, and I want you to trust me and depend on me just like you're teaching Dane to trust and depend on you. In the midst of your worst thoughts and behaviors, I will pursue you with my love. You are mine! I will always love you no matter what."

I thought about the times in my life when I tried so hard to maintain control. I was a real-life superwoman trying to be so strong through all of this, but it was like God was teaching me that my need to be in control was really fear and a lack of trust in him. I was wearing myself out trying to be strong. I'd always lived my life thinking I had to be strong. In fact, relying on my own strength was and is one of my greatest weaknesses. During that season of desperation, when I was so stressed and fearful, I'd hear that mantra playing in my head,

"Who's in charge, Debbie?"

I'd take a deep breath. "You are, God."

"Some of the time or all of the time?"

"You are in charge all of the time, God."

And I was learning to truly mean it and live it. God was the authority in my life—period. He is sovereign and he directs my steps as it says in Proverbs 16:9, "The mind of man plans his way, but the LORD directs his steps."

I thought he had been my authority before, but I realized in those days that I had only partially yielded control of my life to him. I still wanted a big chunk of the control over my life as far as where I worked, how I spent my days, how my kids turned out, what my marriage was like, even how I spent time with him and what areas of ministry I was a part of. I wanted control over those things. The uncertainty of how any of that was going to end up caused me to unequivocally relinquish control to him.

I was beginning to grasp that if I could see the "real boy" inside Dane, God certainly saw the "real girl" within all of my mess, and I felt childishly safe in his care. I knew God was with me through every second of this journey and that he really was my adoptive daddy. Everything he had in store for me was for my good and his purpose, no matter how it seemed to me in my limited understanding.

The long days alone with Dane at home felt kind of like my own personal wilderness experience. It was God and me against Dane's history of harm and neglect. He would provide my strength one day at a time, and during the toughest times, one moment at a time. I had to rely on him to get me through every millisecond of each day. I thought about how in the wilderness the Israelites had to depend on God alone. He gave them food for only one day at a time. They'd been given a promise of a land flowing with milk and honey, but what were they learning in the wilderness? They were learning to depend on him and trust him. And every time they acted in unbelief, they wandered around the desert again (Exodus 16:25-35).

What lessons did I learn in my wilderness experience? I learned dependence on God. I learned that he can be trusted in the midst of my greatest doubts. I learned that his passion was a relationship with me and for me to be deeply connected to him. Just like on Dane's home intervention, it wasn't really about the behavior—although a lot needed to change—but it was about the relationship. As Dr. Cross often taught, "Relationship-based trauma can only be healed in the context of relationship." Many of those days I wanted to get down on my hands and knees and beg Dane to trust me, but he could only learn by becoming dependent on me. My deep trust in God was also learned by utter dependence on him.

I once heard a great sermon on the wilderness while visiting a friend's church. The pastor said it is in the wilderness that God's Word is tested in us. God is testing to see if his Word has taken root. He is testing whether we believe his Word for our own lives and will trust him. In my desperation, I learned to take God at his Word and trust him in the midst of my worst pain and fear.

God clearly let me see that Dane was not the only one with some trust issues. I often acted much like a spiritual orphan. I had an adoptive heavenly daddy, but I was so afraid he wouldn't take care of me, so I had to take care of myself. I was so afraid my family would not survive. His Word continually told me to trust him, but when my circumstances became overwhelming, I didn't believe him. Perhaps I also needed an environment of *frequency, intensity, and duration* with my heavenly daddy. God had my full attention during our home-based intervention and the time had been set aside for his restorative work in my life for whatever reason.

I felt like I'd been given the privilege of unconditionally loving Dane so that I could get a glimpse of how much God loves us in our brokenness. He knows that underlying our maladaptive behaviors, self-reliance, disbelief, and mistrust are the fear and pain of a hurting child. Why else would the Bible repeatedly say to not fear or be afraid? But that will have to be another book.

I had to come to him in that childlike faith. I was safe with God, and I was falling deeper in love with him, realizing that nothing I could ever do or think would separate me from him, because he loved me with a love that would never give up. I was his adopted child. My legal status was changed at the time of my salvation, and I became part of his forever family. When he looks at me, he sees the righteousness of Christ. The price has been paid for my sin, and he sees Christ in me.

But what does it say? "THE WORD IS NEAR YOU, IN YOUR MOUTH AND IN YOUR HEART"-that is, the word of faith which we are preaching, that if you confess with your mouth Jesus as Lord, and believe in your heart that God raised Him from the dead, you will be saved; for with the heart a person believes, resulting in righteousness, and with the mouth he confesses, resulting in salvation. For the Scripture says, "WHOEVER BELIEVES IN HIM WILL NOT BE DISAPPOINTED."

For there is no distinction between Jew and Greek; for the same Lord is Lord of all, abounding in riches for all who call on Him; for "WHOEVER WILL CALL ON THE NAME OF THE LORD WILL BE SAVED." Romans 10:8-13

I developed an insatiable hunger to truly attach to him and trust him like I never had before. Really trust him. Really know him and hear him. Talk to him all the time, not just in a scheduled time I'd set apart early in the morning, but relating to him throughout my whole day and turning to him in the big things and the small things. I needed to learn to listen more. After all, in a relationship, it shouldn't be only one person doing all the talking. I wanted to ask him about everything, just like I would ask Alan if he were standing beside me—a real relationship, not a religious experience. In this more connected walk with God, I could let go of my fears, and he was there to get me through any of my doubts about him because I ultimately knew how much he loved me.

Reading God's Word became relational and conversational, more like I was discussing it with him and being real with him. I'd read a passage and say, "What did you mean by that?" or in some of my Old Testament reading, I'd say, "That was pretty harsh! I'm thankful I get to be under the new covenant." Understanding came to my mind, making scriptures clearer to me than ever before. Sometimes I was shocked at his answers. One time I asked again why he had allowed all the starving orphans in the world, and I immediately heard in my mind, "Why do you?" Ouch! All throughout scripture there are instructions for God's people to care for those in need (Deuteronomy 10:18-19; Deuteronomy 14:29; Psalm 82:3-4; Proverbs 18:17; Isaiah 1:17; Zechariah 7:9-10; Matthew 25:34-40; James 1:27). And that's just a few of the verses. Am I doing my part to feed the poor, visit the lonely, care for those who are sick? Or would I rather go shopping for a new necklace to complement some cute outfit? Be prepared that if you want to know God's heart, he'll show you.

He also showed me a more compassionate love for others. Understanding people became easier. I wanted to love others more like he loves. I saw the fear and pain that lay beneath the behavior and wanted to love them in a way that demonstrated God's love, not act like someone who had it all figured out because I was a Christian. How many times in my life had I turned to something less than healthy instead of trusting God? I wanted everyone to know that we love him because he first loved us (1 John 4:19). How could I help them feel safe so that they could experience the love of God through Christ, then cry out to him and begin to heal? If they could only see how much he loves them and wants them to be part of his kingdom, his forever family.

My spiritual adoption made so much more sense to me now. I studied the familiar scriptures.

> But when the fullness of the time came, God sent forth His Son, born of a woman, born under the Law, so that He might redeem those who were under the Law, that we might receive the adoption as sons. Because you are sons, God has sent forth the Spirit of His Son into our hearts, crying, "Abba! Father!" Therefore you are no longer a slave, but a son; and if a son, then an heir through God. Galatians 4. 4-7

Pretty awesome! Why did God have a plan to redeem us? So that he could adopt us! We are chosen children, part of his forever family through our faith in Christ. We cry out to him, "Abba, Father." Abba is an Aramaic word and was commonly used by small children in addressing their fathers. It is intimate, yet respectful. It closely translates as "papa" or "daddy." It was the cry of Jesus to God as he hung on the cross (Mark 14:36).

As God's child, I cried out to him in desperation. I screamed out to him when it looked like I'd have to send Dane away. He heard my cry. He sent wise people to instruct us. He sent loving people to help us and guide us in the midst of our pain and trauma. His eyes never left us, although in our earthly time frame, it seemed his answers were quite delayed. "I will instruct you and teach you in the way which you should go; I will counsel you with My eye upon you" (Psalm 32:8).

I didn't know at the time where all of this was headed and didn't understand why my family had gone through this type of testing, but I knew for certain that my heavenly father was on my side as a loving parent, and no loving parent would lead his child to harm. A loving parent leads his child to healing and wholeness. He was up to something big here, and it had to do with my heart more than it had to do with this home intervention. It had to do with the simple message of the gospel: "For God so loved the world, that He gave His only begotten Son, that whoever believes in Him should not perish, but have eternal life" (John 3:16).

He loved us so much that he did the unthinkable to bring us home with him. Do you really know how much God loves you? I mean really loves you, more than moms and dads love their own children? Do you truly get that he would do anything to have a relationship with you? Do you know that no matter what rebellious acts or thoughts you've had, that he wants you to be his own? You can't mess up badly enough for him to not want you. You can't run far enough for him to not chase you down. He would do anything-anything but violate your will- for you to be his adopted child. He would do anything to make you whole and set you free from all that torments you. And he did. He sent Jesus. All we have to do is believe like a little child and receive him.

That's it! Simple, childlike faith in Jesus and a redemptive plan that a mighty, sovereign, holy, loving God wanted to adopt us and give us his kingdom, not only in the life to come, but in this life that we live on earth. He adopted us for relationship, for our freedom, and for our healing. And even when life throws us a curve that we cannot make sense of, he has a purpose for us. He is not a mean God, but a healing parent.

Chapter 11
. . . .
Today in Our Journey

Our journey of becoming healing parents had many ups and downs, twists and turns. I am often concerned that my testimony might discourage others from adopting. That it is not the intent of this book and certainly not a reflection of my heart. It is my heart that adoptive parents will find answers earlier in their journey and that if you are considering adoption, you will apply the trust-based parenting strategies from the very beginning and avoid some of the mistakes we made. When I spoke to a group of parents recently, I said, "My advice to you when your child comes home is this: Don't take 'em to Disneyland and do come out of Denial-land. Quickly!"

Educate yourself on the effects of early harm and learn all you can about brain development, neurochemistry, sensory processing, and attachment. Clear your calendar and structure your days around meeting the needs of an infant, even if that child is in a much older body. Do not be so quick in wanting to catch them up that you bypass important developmental milestones.

People have sometimes asked me the "If you had to do it all over again" question. My answer: "Do what? Obey God? Yes, I would." I never doubted and don't doubt now that Alan and I were called to adopt Dane. He is our son. We'll love him forever. I am a huge advocate of adoption, and I don't ever want our story to scare parents out of God's call on their lives. That being said, I am a huge advocate of informed adoption.

Children from backgrounds of abandonment, neglect, abuse, or other trauma have fear-based and pain-based issues that need to be handled much differently than traditional parenting, even traditional Christian parenting. Parents must be educated and trained so that they approach their new sons and daughters with compassionate understanding about their unique, challenging, and often confusing behaviors.

We struggled so long before we found correct answers and in retrospect, there are so many things we would have done differently. We now have an opportunity to help other parents on similar journeys, and it is our hope that sharing our story will help others have a less difficult path.

To be quite blunt and honest, there's no way I would have gone through this much pain and suffering to help others, but Christ would have, and as believers we are being conformed into the image of Christ (Romans 8:29). Somehow, in the big scheme of things, God allowed an adoption journey to be part of my becoming more conformed to the image of Christ. I've still got a long way to go; just ask Alan and my kids!

I don't know anyone who hasn't been through some testing and trials on the journey of becoming more like Christ. Our suffering is so mild compared to what he suffered, yet as fellow believers, our suffering can be used to not only help others in their suffering, but to give a testimony to the restorative work of a mighty God.

Just last week, I had the privilege of meeting and hearing Don Piper, author of *90 Minutes in Heaven.* Don endured some suffering! He died in a car wreck, was dead for ninety minutes, saw the glory of heaven, and came back to life in a body that had to be put back together through many months of agonizing pain, surgeries, and years of never being the same. He has touched countless lives through sharing his story, and he gives all the glory to God. My favorite thing he said in his speech was, "Turn your test into a testimony, your mess into a message."

Our family's mess is now our message. Our journey with Dane and his continuing story of restoration led me to form PACT: Parenting Adoptees Can Trust, whose mission is to provide education, support, and research-based strategies to help parents of foster, adoptive, and at-risk children build better relationships with their children.

Karyn is now Dr. Karyn Purvis, and she has spent the last several years speaking all over the world to parents, professionals, and adoption ministries. She and Dr. David Cross are now directors of The TCU Institute of Child Development and have formalized their years of research into a parenting model called Trust-Based Relational Intervention® (TBRI®). I often refer to it as Trust-based parenting. Information about this, PACT, and other resources for parents may be found in the resource list.

A few years ago a passage in Isaiah just jumped all over me.

Do not fear, for I have redeemed you;
I have called you by name; you are Mine!
When you pass through the waters, I will be with you;
And through the rivers, they will not overflow you.
When you walk through the fire, you will not be scorched,
Nor will the flame burn you.
For I am the Lord your God,
The Holy One of Israel, your Savior. Isaiah 43:1b-3a

These verses gave me Holy Ghost goose bumps all over my arms as I remembered God telling me so clearly during that wilderness season when I was home with Dane, "You are mine!"

I know am his, just like Megan is mine and Dane is mine, no matter who carried him in her womb. Verse 2 of this passage didn't say "if" you go through the waters, it said "when," but God promises to be with me. It didn't say "if" you walk through the fire, it said "when" you walk through the fire, but God promises I will not be scorched. He is with me, and I can only conclude that if he allowed painful circumstances in my life, if he purified me as though with fire, he will use it for his purpose and his kingdom. He will do the same for you, in whatever you are going through in this season of your life that caused you to pick up a book entitled, *God, Are You Nice or Mean?* Trust him.

May your journey be precious, both with your loved ones and in trusting the one who first loved you.

Blessed be the God and Father of our Lord Jesus Christ, the Father of mercies and God of all comfort; who comforts us in all our affliction so that we may be able to comfort those who are in any affliction with the comfort with which we ourselves are comforted by God. For just as the sufferings of Christ are ours in abundance, so also our comfort is abundant through Christ. 2 Corinthians 1: 3-5

Resources

Websites:

PACT: Parenting Adoptees Can Trust, directed by Debra Delulio Jones, M Ed
http://www.parentingadopteescantrust.com

The TCU Institute of Child Development, directed by Dr. Karyn Purvis and Dr. David Cross
http://www.child.tcu.edu

Empowered to Connect – adoption and foster care resources, Dr. Karyn Purvis with Michael and Amy Monroe
http://www.empoweredtoconnect.org

Child Trauma Academy, directed by Dr. Bruce Perry, M.D., Ph. D.
http://www.childtrauma.org

Deborah D. Gray – specializing in attachment, grief, and trauma issues
http://www.deborahdgray.com

Attach – Association for Treatment and Training in the Attachment of Children
http://www.attach.org

Dr. Mary Ann Block, Medical director and top-selling author
http://www.blockcenter.com

Dr. Doris Rapp, Board-certified environmental medical specialist and pediatric allergist
http://www.drrapp.com

The Out-of-Sync Child, Carol Stock Kranowitz, M.A.
http://www.out-of-sync-child.com

Sensory Processing Disorder Foundation
http://www.spdfoundation.net

Sensory Processing Disorder Resource Center
http://www.sensory-processing-disorder.com

The Therapy Shoppe – an assortment of therapy merchandise and specialty toys and games
http://www.therapyshoppe.com

The Theraplay® Institute – building strong families and emotionally healthy children
http://www.theraplay.org

The Alert Program – clearly defined steps for teaching
self-regulation awareness
http://www.alertprogram.com

Infant Massage – bonding with your baby through infant
massage
http://www.babybabyohbaby.com

Weighted Blankets – the natural aid for sensory relaxation
and restful sleep
http://www.weightedblanket.net

Fetal Alcohol Syndrome Consultation, Education, and
Training Services, Inc
http://www.fascets.org

Special Education Law
http://wrightslaw.com

Tapestry Adoption and Foster Care Ministry at Irving
Bible Church
http://www.tapestryministry.org

Show Hope – Shaohannah's Hope: A Movement to Care
for Orphans
http://www.showhope.org

Christian Alliance for Orphans – unites more than 100
respected Christian organizations committed to adoption,
foster care, and global orphan care

http://www.christian-alliance-for-orphans.org

Together for Adoption – provides gospel-centered resources to mobilize the church for global orphan care
http://www.togetherforadoption.org

Hope for Orphans – A ministry of FAMILYLIFE® – serving every church to reach every orphan
http://hopefororphans.org

Embrace – the church reclaiming the care of orphans and waiting children
http://www.embracetexas.org

Saddleback Church Orphan Care – Southern California
http://www.saddleback.com/aboutsaddleback/signatureministries/orphancare

Alliance 14:18 – Greater Houston Alliance for the Fatherless
http://www.alliance1418.com

Books:

Block, Dr. Mary Ann, *No More Ritalin: Treating ADHD Without Drugs*, (Kensington Publishing Corp., 1996).

Gray, Deborah D., *Attaching in Adoption: Practical Tools for Today's Parents*, (Perspectives Press, Inc., 2002).

Gray, Deborah D., *Nurturing Adoptions: Creating Resilience after Neglect and Trauma*, (Perspectives Press, Inc., 2007).

Karen, Robert, Ph.D., *Becoming Attached: First Relationships and How They Shape Our Capacity to Love*, (Oxford University Press, 1994).

Kranowitz, Carol Stock, M.A. and Lucy Jane Miller, Ph. D., OTR, *The Out-of-Sync Child: Recognizing and Coping with Sensory Processing Disorder, Revised Edition*, (Penguin Group, Inc., 2005).

Kranowitz, Carol Stock, M.A., *The Out-of-Sync Child Has Fun, Revised Edition: Activities for Kids with Sensory Processing Disorder*, (Penguin Group, Inc., 2006).

Perry, Bruce D., M.D., Ph.D. and Maia Szalavitz, *The Boy Who Was Raised as a Dog: And Other Stories from a Child Psychiatrist's Notebook–What Traumatized Children Can Teach Us About Loss, Love and Healing*, (Basic Books, 2006).

Perry, Bruce D., M.D., Ph.D. and Maia Szalavitz, *Born for Love: Why Empathy is Essential–and Endangered*, (HarperCollins Publishers, 2011).

Piper, Don and Cecil Murphey, *90 Minutes in Heaven: A True Story of Life and Death*, (Revell, a division of Baker Publishing Group, 2004).

Purvis, Karyn B., Ph.D., David R. Cross, Ph. D., and Wendy Lyons Sunshine, *The Connected Child: Bring Hope and Healing to Your Adoptive Family*, (McGraw-Hill, 2007).

Purvis, Dr. Karyn with Michael and Amy Monroe, *Created to Connect: A Christian's Guide to The Connected Child*, (Empowered to Connect™, 2010, free downloadable pdf file at http://www.empoweredtoconnect.org/guide).

Rapp, Doris J., M.D., *Is This Your Child*, (William Morrow and Company, Inc., 1992).

Siegel, Daniel, M.D. and Mary Hartzell, M.Ed., *Parenting From the Inside Out*, (Penguin Group Inc., 2003).

Siegel, Daniel, M.D. and Tina Payne Bryson, Ph.D., *The Whole-Brain Child: 12 Revolutionary Stragtegies to Nurture Your Child's Developing Mind*, (Delacorte Press, 2011).

DVD (all available from The TCU Institute of Child Development, http://www.child.tcu.edu/DVD%20sales.asp)

Healing Family Series:

Trust-Based Parenting: Creating Lasting Changes in Your Child's Behaviors

A Sensory World: Making Sense of Sensory Disorders

Playful Interaction

Healthy Touch

(a new DVD on attachment will soon be available in this series)

Lecture Series:

Empowering, Connecting & Correcting Principles

The Attachment Dance

Facilitating Behavioral Change

Healing Research

Sensory Integration

The Neurochemistry of Fear

Texas Judicial Summit:

2009 Texas Judicial Summit: Improving Outcomes for Children in Care